BREAKING TI

The Key to Recovering Self-Esteem

Rachael Clyne

"Inspiring, practical and wise. This is an essential book for anyone seeking to understand and heal low self-esteem. I'm sure it will help many people."
Dr William Bloom

"I feel fantastic about myself, I love being me at the moment, I wouldn't be anyone else. I'm less self-absorbed, no longer preoccupied with imagining what others are thinking."

"I haven't had any negative thoughts, since I started saying No! and refused to let them in. They've just gone; they simply haven't arisen. I can't believe how easy it's been and that I could change things in less than a week. Perhaps I just needed permission to say No!"

"I'm able to banish negative thinking and stay away from people who are bad for my mental health."

These and other quotes from clients in this book are anonymous and have been used with the permission of the client.

other books by the same author

Cancer Your Life -Your Choice

BREAKING THE SPELL

The Key to Recovering Self-Esteem

Rachael Clyne

PS AVALON
Glastonbury, England

First published in the U.K. in 2005 by PS Avalon

PS Avalon
Box 1865, Glastonbury
Somerset, BA6 8YR, U.K.
www.psavalon.com

revised edition 4/2005

Rachael Clyne asserts the moral right
to be identified as the author of this work

Cartoons: Rachael Clyne

Back cover photo: Collette Barnard

Design: Will Parfitt

ISBN 0-9544764-5-X

Contents

About the Author

Rachael Clyne is a psychotherapist and counsellor, author and artist, living in Glastonbury. She has had a long- term interest in what is commonly known as Addiction Recovery Work and in particular, recovery from co-dependence. Co-dependence concerns dysfunctional and addictive forms of relating and sufferers often have low self-esteem. She has worked in addiction recovery centres and in particular in a unit for women, where residents frequently suffered from chronic low self-esteem as a result of neglect, abuse and devastating loss.

Rachael has run a wide range of personal development groups and counselling training courses, including groups based on the ideas presented in the book. She has had public exhibitions of her installation work in London and around the country. She is also a published poet and priestess of Avalon.

Following her husband's illness with cancer in 1983, she left her career as a professional actress to become involved with counselling cancer patients and founded London's first cancer support group. Her first book called "Cancer Your Life - Your Choice" (Thorsons 1986), aimed to bridge the differences between alternative and orthodox approaches to cancer treatment.

Rachael then went on to train in Psychosynthesis, an approach to psychotherapy that emphasises the creative and the spiritual. In 1986 she established a private practice, and has worked with individuals and groups since then.

Acknowledgements

To my teachers and sources of inspiration: Elaine Harrison, who nurtured faith in my creativity. Betty Balcombe whose unique humour and steadfastness saw me through some very difficult times. Christina Feldman, for her humorous words of wisdom and humanity. Pia Mellody, for her honesty, clarity and generosity. Diana Whitmore, for her recognition of my spirit. Jill Gabriel, for her consistent love and support. Kathy Jones, for creating the space for me to express my priestess-self. To the Nine Morgens and all the wise, loving beings who nudged me along the wisdom road. To my family and all my good friends, especially Geoff & Carole Windham and Collette Barnard who have enabled me to feel known and loved through the years despite myself. To Will Parfitt, my friend and publisher, without whom this book would not have got into print. To my clients who inspire and continue to teach me, and to those who generously allowed me to quote their words and stories. A special thank-you to the Women of Pathway who tested and taught me what it means to struggle from the rock-bottom of life and gave me the opportunity to be a Warrior of the Heart with them.

This book is dedicated to all who struggle to re-find that sense of self which allows us to live with dignity, respect and love.

May we all be freed from self-hatred
May all beings everywhere be freed from despair
May we all live with love
May all beings everywhere find peace
Blessed Be

Introduction

What matters is that we stop hating ourselves; when we do so what has to replace it is Love!

Much of this book comes from my own struggles and journey and much from the experience of working with others. It has become my passion to teach people how to stop hating themselves and let the natural state of love shine through. In my darkest moments of despair and self-hatred I used a particular meditation practice which reminded me that whatever I was feeling, in that very moment there must be hundreds of thousands of people across the planet experiencing the same pain. Recognising this fact broke my sense of isolation and helped me transcend my own suffering to a place of compassion. It enabled me to make positive use of the negativity I was experiencing as a prayer for us all. Little did I think that the memory of those moments when I thought I was most stuck would stay with me as critical turning points in my own journey. Breaking the Spell is as much a personal sharing as it is a self-help book and is a natural expression of that prayer.

My journey has been a long process of recovery from low self-worth to a sense of self that is solid, resilient and affirming. It is a journey that has led me through various routes; personal therapy, Buddhist Meditation, Feminist Goddess Spirituality, Twelve Step Recovery work, personal creativity through writing and artwork and the hard lessons learned through intimate relationships.

For the most part I have functioned in life, I have always done work that has fulfilled me, I have friends and I have a rich inner life. I am fortunate in having a wealth of creativity and spirit to draw upon. On the surface I appeared bright and confident, but for much of my life, that confidence was a defensive front that hid a chronic underlying insecurity and lack of esteem. My first career was as a stage and television actress, a career that continually demands and knocks one's confidence and I developed a supreme ability to "act" with confidence. There are many reasons in my background and in my personality that made it hard for me to develop self-esteem. I was loved, my gifts and talents were encouraged and lauded, but "me the child" was neglected. My parents' own lack of self-esteem was such that they were unable to provide me with a sense of self-worth or acquaint me with the skills of how to give it to myself. In addition, there are certain elements in my cultural background, personality and lifestyle, which have put me outside conventional norms and have made it much harder for me to feel acceptable.

Lack of self-esteem has cost me in relationships, health, income and career, as well as loss of joy and quality of life. It has led me into unhealthy dependencies and destructive relationships. It has meant frequent periods of depression and despair when simply getting through the day was a feat of endurance. Low self-esteem has led me to feel the deep pain of shame at not being able to stand up for myself at times when I knew others were taking advantage or mistreating me. It has made me needy and demanding of friends and partners as I tried to get them to help plug up the hole inside me.

Working with clients has perhaps been my most constant source of learning, teaching and testing the ideas and methods I have formed, and I acknowledge how much of a privilege and inspiration it is to be able to do so. It has also, at times, been extremely challenging, especially with those people who have suffered intolerable levels of damage to their sense of self and worth. For a while I worked with women recovering from drug and alcohol addiction in a residential treatment centre. This group of clients present the most challenging of behaviour, lack of trust, aggression, self-harm, manipulation, and deceit. Whilst much of their behaviour relates to the consequences of prolonged substance abuse, it invariably stems from chronic low self-esteem and self-hatred. The road to recovery for these clients is hard and fraught with failures and it requires tremendous courage, faith and persistence. But, when it works nothing can surpass the triumph of a woman who was once at the rock bottom of life and who is now starting to blossom with a new-found pride and love she is finally able to experience for herself.

Recently I have been using my approach with clients in GP Surgeries and with great success. This is short-term counselling work with patients receiving up to six sessions. I am amazed that what took me years is being achieved in two, or three sessions in some cases. The people I have quoted throughout the book have been plagued by lack of confidence and poor self image for years, some as a result of abusive relationships. For some it is a matter of having the right information and acquiring the skills needed to halt the habit of low self-esteem. This automatically creates a sense of encouragement and of being in charge of one's life and very soon people catch onto the means of increasing and maintaining their self-esteem.

One of the most frequent reasons people seek help from a counsellor or therapist, is lack of self-esteem. Lack of self-worth is found in all areas of society. Poverty is more than a material condition; emotional deprivation and poverty of spirit can be found in the most outwardly successful, as well as the socially disadvantaged. Low self-esteem can be the driving force of ambition or the obstacle to it. It can be found in the silent everyday experience of those around us who appear quiet and caring; it can be hidden behind the bravura of the extravert and beneath the aggressive behaviour of the bully. So often our self-esteem is invested in and dependent upon what we DO, or what we HAVE, rather than upon WHO WE ARE. We base it on our work, our money, our relationships, or our role as parents. When Life strips these away, the solidity and authenticity of our sense of self is tested.

Lack of self-esteem is a frequent cause of depression, anxiety, addiction, and emotional dysfunction. So why is it that some people seem to be able to be confident, stay calm and stand up for themselves, while others, feel worthless, powerless, ashamed, to blame, guilty?

Some people have suffered abuse and violence, and have strong reasons to fear being themselves. Some have grown up in an environment where others around them suffered from low esteem and they were simply not shown how to behave in a way that creates a healthy sense of self. Other people may have aspects of their cultural background, personality, sexuality or lifestyle, which place them in a social minority making it harder for them to feel acceptable.

Most people with low self-esteem believe they need to improve themselves in order to gain self-esteem. In fact they are continually working on it, driving themselves, berating and punishing themselves in an attempt to earn self- esteem. In effect what they are doing is maintaining a system of low self-esteem. One could argue that low-self esteem is in itself a destructive attempt to achieve it.

What we do not often realise is that low self-esteem is a form of self-abuse. We think we are being non-violent by turning guilt and anger onto ourselves. People with low self-esteem often have an abhorrence of abuse but do not recognise that mentally and emotionally beating themselves up is abusive.

People usually think that they have to feel better about themselves before they can find self-esteem. In fact it works the other way round. Once we make a decision to stop being violent towards ourselves, we then automatically start to feel better about ourselves. Self-esteem is largely the ability to refuse to be undermined, and when we begin to create self-respect we naturally start to experience love.

We have to prepare the ground for building self-esteem, to clear a space before we can nurture ourselves. Unless we learn to stop the self-defeating attitudes and behaviours that maintain worthlessness, all our attempts at positive reinforcement and esteem building techniques will amount to nothing. We simply will not be able to let them in.

We have to make a choice to feel good about ourselves exactly the way we are. That choice comes with the recognition that self-esteem is a fundamental right. It is at the core of our human dignity. Just as we need to be able to talk and walk in order to function physically, so we need to be able to feel good about ourselves in order to function psychologically.

This book has its own unique angle on a popular topic and aims to put its ideas across in a direct and accessible manner. Breaking the Spell is about understanding how self-esteem operates. It seeks to uncover the systems of negative and punitive thinking and behaviour by which we maintain low self-esteem. It offers ways of breaking these destructive behaviour patterns and provides suggestions for creating a healthier and more loving sense of self. I believe that when we learn to stop hating ourselves, what has to replace it is Love.

Each chapter builds the journey, step by step, from low self-esteem to a sense of self worth that can be consolidated and can thrive. The chapters contain exercises for you to use and suggestions for rewarding yourself for having reached the end of the chapter. It is up to you whether or not you do the exercises, some people like to have things to do, others just like to read and take in the ideas. There is also a book list of at the end of the book.

Most people who lack esteem believe they are selfish, weak or ugly; in fact they are usually loving, caring and generous. The trouble is they just do not seem able to extend that love and generosity to themselves.

Proud

And when I am nothing
Like a little lost childseed
Waitin' in de dark belly
I go down to de sea
Yemaya eh! Yemaya eh!
Mother Ocean help me!

An she say,
"You woman you proud!
You woman you proud!
You is de sea
You is de rock
You is de grass

You is de tree

Take me into your child place
Take me into your belly
Take me into your heart
And let de sing come out!"

And de wave she rise me all de way up to my heart
And me sing
Me woman me proud, me woman me proud
Me proud, me proud, me proud!

1

What Is Self-Esteem?

Self-esteem is about having a basic love and respect for ourselves and our right to be here with all our faults and attributes; our warts and our wings. It contains both acceptance of our humanity and pride in our potential. Self-esteem does not have to be earned, it is independent of achievement or behaviour; just being alive and being who we are is enough. We deserve the best simply because we are. We are neither better nor worse than other people; we are equal and different. Self-esteem helps us to demand respect, it gives us the confidence to stand up for ourselves and to go out in the world. It enables us to take responsibility for our actions without wracking ourselves with needless guilt and shame.

Self-esteem is expressed through our ability to refuse to be put down; it gives us resilience, a sense of joy and love for ourselves that can withstand the knocks of life. It is like a warm smile in the belly with which we can reassure ourselves when times are tough. It is a tenderness in the heart that embraces us when we are hurt. Self-esteem is our own well of being that we can draw from when we are thirsty or tired. Self -esteem allows us to enjoy our own company and enables us to recognise that we are our own best friend. For these reasons, people with self-esteem are often good people to be around, they have a sense of joy, resilience and empowerment that is infectious.

How Self-Esteem Develops

If you observe an infant, invariably she or he expresses a joy and aliveness that seems irrepressible. They do not question their right to be here, they show little shame or inhibition in expressing their needs, rather they yell when they are hungry, tired or needing some attention. Smile at an infant and it readily returns your smile, they love to be the centre of attention, they are curious, spontaneous and fearless. Infants are uninhibited about their bodies, their bodily functions and mess, they are naturally affectionate and trusting. If we consider all this we could say that self-esteem is our natural state, so how does this change?

As infants we are utterly dependent upon others for our survival and we are deeply affected by how our world responds to us, how it reflects back to us our sense of existence. As infants we have little sense of separateness from our Mother figure or our surroundings, we are merged with them. It is through the responses, the reflections and the affirmations we receive that we can begin to develop a sense of our individual existence. When we gurgle does Mummy smile and mimic our gurgling sounds? Through her mirroring we know we have an impact, we know we have made a sound that can be heard. When we cry to be picked up, or fed, does someone respond positively? It is through these positive affirmations that we begin to build a confidence and robustness in our ability to exist and survive as separate beings. We are sensitive to the tiniest of nuances, voice-tones, gestures and actions.

If we are not responded to we can experience a sense of powerlessness over our own survival, a doubt in our own existence. How able are we to make Mother's breast available when we need it? How able are we to fulfil our need to be held when we cry for it? If we are not, we experience ourselves abandoned in some existential limbo, in a lost and uncertain universe.

As we become toddlers we start to explore our world and experiment with brief periods of separation. This is tolerable as long as we can trust that Mummy or Daddy will still be there when we need them. We create substitutes to help us through those moments; teddy bears, blankets, transitional objects which symbolise the love and comfort of Mummy. We learn to internalise that self-image. As we first learn to walk, we wobble, as we first learn to hold an image of ourselves we also wobble. Eventually we are able to sustain a stable and loving enough image of ourselves to manage longer periods of separation.

It is in our earliest years that our core self-esteem is formed but it continues to be consolidated through each stage of development. The responses and messages of those around us continue to have an impact on our sense of worth especially interactions with parents, or other family members such as siblings. School years and education have a major influence on us, how we feel about learning, how successfully we interact with our fellow pupils and with authority figures; all play their part. Puberty and adolescence represent the forming of our sexual identity and threshold into adulthood. How we ride the hormonal changes and relate to our growing bodies is another key aspect in the development of self-esteem. Each stage presents its challenges and contributes to our sense of self-worth.

Even if we had what we needed at the start of our lives, we may encounter later experiences which fracture the connection with that original sense of our own goodness. Perhaps we lost a parent through death or divorce. We might have moved home and lost our bearings, our friends, or our sense of familiarity. Maybe we experienced loss of confidence in our intellectual ability, or our body image and desirability. As teenagers we are often acutely sensitive to our self-image and peer approval. Being cool, fitting the conventions of attractiveness, having the right clothes, the right girl/boyfriend etc all take on enormous importance and it can be a time when self-esteem is most tested and most vulnerable.

Being told we are special and that we are fine as we are, being praised for our attempts and encouraged in our interests, gives us confidence. Being listened to, being held and told that we are loved, being respected as a person in our own right; all these messages help to reinforce our sense of self. Being set clear and healthy limits, against which we can test ourselves, helps us to feel held. It enables us to develop self-respect and the ability to contain ourselves. Overtly negative messages such as being told we are stupid, ugly, or unwanted clearly make us doubt our self-worth, especially when repeatedly given. Indirect messages through lack of response, neglect and lack of affection or attention are equally powerful.

Another important aspect of developing a healthy sense of self comes from clear definition of roles. In other words, as children we are the "child" and our parent remains the "parent". As long as the adult carer remains the "parent" we have someone to depend upon, to test ourselves against, to feel held by. If the parent is insecure and dependent themselves the roles can get reversed and they may habitually lean on their child for comfort and support. In this way the child then becomes the carer attending to the needs of the dependent adult. This role reversal can give the child a sense of importance and of being needed, but at the cost of its own needs which are neglected. It leads a child to have an overdeveloped sense of responsibility and a poor sense of their own innate worth.

Being expected to achieve, to perform, to behave well, to please in order to gain approval teaches us to have a false-self, a persona, whilst the real "us" remains invisible and unacceptable. Children who are gifted intellectually or artistically can sometimes find it hard to reconcile the gap between their gifted selves and the ordinary child. A shining ability in Maths or Music does not necessarily assume the same ability in emotional literacy or social relating.

We learn so much of how to be from the behaviour modelled by our parent figures. If our parents seem stable, with a strong sense of who they are, we are able to internalise that experience. When we see a parent take upsets in their stride, without panicking, we take in the message that we too do not have to be anxious when things go wrong. If we see a parent act with self-respect we learn that it is ok to stand up for ourselves. If they show that it is ok to make mistakes, we will be more willing to accept our own. If they are fearful or ashamed of being themselves, we will tend to adopt the same attitudes and believe that this is the way to be! Even if we recognise that it is not, we are frustrated by a lack of the role model to enable us to behave otherwise. If our parents react to every upset by anticipating the worst, we too will learn to be fearful.

Self-esteem can be solid and it can also be variable, as we experience relatively high self-esteem in some areas in our life, whilst in others we find ourselves to be more vulnerable. So many of us invest our self-esteem in our work, our money, or our role as parent and partner. When Life strips away these props, as it is prone to do, then we are tested to see just how real and solid our confidence is. The influences on our sense of self-esteem are many and complex, but once a pattern becomes established it has a habit of reinforcing itself. Through our expectations and our fears we unconsciously attract and seek experiences which conform to those expectations. We interpret events through the filter of our memories and associations, forming conclusions that confirm our beliefs, whether or not they accurately reflect what is happening in the present.

If we have developed a sense of self and worth that is negative, it is possible to change. We need to uncover and recognise the beliefs and the behaviours that create and maintain it. We have to deal with the feelings and fears that stop us from allowing ourselves a positive self-image. We have to acquire and practice the attitudes and behaviours that generate self-love, self-respect, confidence and all the other qualities contained in self-esteem. First we may need to recognise the characteristics, the behaviour and attitudes that express self-esteem.

Signs of Self-esteem

Which of the following signs do you identify with? You may find you experience esteem in some areas, but not others. Start to define how your self-esteem operates.

1 Having a sense of self-acceptance and confidence that does not need to prove itself. Whether we are shy and unassuming, loud and extravert, rich or poor, we trust that however we are and whoever we are, is ok. ❑

2 Being able to please ourselves. We do not have to constantly adapt ourselves in order to please people, nor do we have to continually drive ourselves to be perfect. ❑

3 Ability to face our shortcomings without letting it demolish our sense of self. It does not mean we are immune to criticism, but are able to acknowledge responsibility for our actions without becoming a victim. ❏

4 Ability to distinguish between what we are responsible for and what we are not. ❏

5 Resilience in the face of setbacks. We recognise that life has setbacks and we are able to face those knocks without taking it personally or blaming ourselves. Even if we do fall prey to negative feelings, to sadness, shame or despair, we do not dwell there. We understand that bad things happen to good people. ❏

6 Having an innate sense of optimism, seeing problems as opportunities for growth and moving on. ❏

7 Having a clear sense of our own reality, what we are feeling and thinking. We are able to distinguish between our own and another's reality. ❏

8 Recognising the need for boundaries, for privacy, discretion. We are able to respect our own and others space. ❏

9 Trusting ourselves and being able to trust others in a healthy way. We usually have a good sense of when to trust others or a situation and when not. ❏

10 Ability to be assertive, to say "No" and "Yes" appropriately. We are able to stand up for ourselves in a clear way. We can also wisely withdraw when necessary, without feeling a failure. We do not need to bully or be a victim. ❏

11 Being able to nurture ourselves, to recognise our limitations and take care of ourselves when we are tired, stressed or ill. We are also able to indulge ourselves and

have fun, without feeling guilty.   ❏

12 Equally, we are able to accept help and support when it is
offered and when it feels appropriate.   ❏

13 Being able to receive compliments and love.   ❏

Signs of Low Self-Esteem

1 Lack of confidence; we imagine everyone else knows
how to do things, be happy, be successful and we don't. We
put ourselves down, even when the reality is that we are
talented and able.   ❏

2 Adapting, sacrificing ourselves to please others, having to
be nice or good.   ❏

3 Having to be perfect. 99% shrinks into insignificance
against that giant 1% that deems us a complete failure. We
are often driven in our need to be perfect, working longer
hours, pouring more of ourselves into a situation than
anyone else. Rarely satisfied when our goals are realised,
we experience only temporary respite from the continual
anxiety that we should be doing more, or doing it better.   ❏

4 Having a deep sense of shame and self-hatred that has to
be hidden from others, believing that, "if they really got to
know me they'd hate me."   ❏

5 Hypersensitivity to criticism or making mistakes, always
believing ourselves to be entirely responsible, to blame.   ❏

6 Emotionally beating ourselves up. Having inner voices
that relentlessly undermine us with such phrases as, "You're
stupid, useless, pathetic."   ❏

7 Having unrealistic expectations. We are very hard on

ourselves and often on others. Alternatively we may be hard on ourselves and too soft with others, making excuses for them when we are let down. After all, they are perfect and we are not. ❏

8 Flipping between worthlessness and grandiosity with aims that are over-ambitious and unrealistic. ❏

9 Perceiving ourselves as victims, expecting the worst from life and from others. When things go wrong it simply proves us right, "I told you so, it always happens to me!" ❏

10 Frequent depression and anxiety. When we fall into a negative state we find it hard to pull ourselves out again. ❏

11 Giving other people's words and thoughts more power than our own, believing that they must be right. We frequently doubt ourselves and that what we have to say is not worth listening to, or will be laughed at. ❏

12 Having poor boundaries, allowing others to invade us easily. Equally, we may be inappropriately invasive with others, or too open, exposing ourselves in an unsafe way. ❏

13 Having a poor sense of trust, either naively trusting people or situations that are unsafe, or behaving in a rejecting or over-controlling manner with those who might support us. ❏

14 Difficulty in asserting or standing up for ourselves. We can fall into placating, isolating ourselves or become frozen with fear. Often we do not even realise that we had the right to stand up for ourselves in a situation until friends point it out to us. In contrast we may over-react with aggression and blame. ❏

15 We may be very needy and demanding, but unable to really receive support. We are like the bottomless bucket that can never be filled. Alternatively, we are unable to voice

our needs, but are resentful and blaming when our needs ☐
are not met.

16 Resistance to nurturing ourselves with a tendency to
deny ourselves when we most need it. ☐

17 Inability to accept compliments, or love; the very things ☐
we crave.

How did you do with this list of experiences? Exact scores are
unimportant, it is the overall balance that counts and it may help
you identify particular areas where you need to build on your
self-esteem and others where you fare better than anticipated.

Activities

Development of Self-Esteem

❖ What messages did you receive from your family, from your
peers, from adults around you? Make a list including both
positive and negative messages and influences.

❖ Who were the positive role models in your life? These may
have been immediate or extended family, friends, teachers.

Reward Yourself with a Strawberry

Well done for looking at the specific details of your self-esteem!
You now deserve a reward and I want you to get into the habit

of rewarding yourself, because it is good for the body as well as mind and spirit.

Strawberries symbolise the sweet things of life, things that make us feel good. They are simple, positive acts of self-affirmation that get the endorphins flowing. Endorphins are the "feel good" chemicals produced by the brain which have a positive effect not only on our psyche but also on our immune system. The author William Bloom in his book, "The Endorphin Effect", uses the word strawberries in this context. Strawberry comes from a traditional Zen Buddhist story about a man who is dangling over the edge of a cliff. At the very moment when all is lost and he is about to plunge to his death, he notices a wild strawberry plant just by his hand. He lets go, plucks the strawberry and treasures the moment, saying "Ah! What a delicious strawberry!" Bloom describes how positive images and acts help to release these "feel good" brain chemicals

You may have been used to rewarding yourself in destructive ways, so this is the chance to start acquiring healthy ways of nurturing yourself. For those of us who are really struggling with self-hate and hopelessness, simply getting up will be a supreme act today. If so just get up and go out, walk for half an hour. A strawberry can be as simple as the smell of fresh coffee, the image of a particular landscape that inspires you, or permission to sit and do nothing for half an hour. It might be spending time with a special friend who affirms and accepts you. Whatever it is, give yourself a strawberry for taking the second step on your road to self-esteem, the first step was buying this book! So take a break, a cup of tea, a walk, or simply a pat on the back for having made this positive step.

2

Why Do We Hang onto Low Self-Esteem?
(even though we know it's bad for us)

"The concept of confidence feels quite strange – I've had none since I was little. Recently I've begun to say what I think at work and colleagues have been shocked and tell me, "That's the most we've ever heard you say.""

Those of us with low self-esteem long for the day when we will finally feel good enough about ourselves, when we will no longer be plagued with the negative thoughts and attitudes that make us believe we are pathetic and worthless. We long to feel loved, wanted, supported and approved of and yet if others try to give us the things we long for we will reject them out of hand. We do not want to listen and often object vehemently to any kind of positive affirmation. It seems crazy that we would reject the very things we are so desperate for, yet this craziness is typical of low self-esteem.

With some clients I have found it is simply a matter of skills and knowing how to change the habits of negative thinking. With these clients major changes have happened within two to six sessions. Once people connect with the approach and use the strategies they experience immediate results, fewer negative thoughts, absence of panic and depression and confidence to act and initiate in ways they never had before. Personally I find it astounding that a lifetime of negativity can be transformed so easily and so quickly. For others it may take much longer for those changes to permeate through the layers and history of their own low self-esteem.

Some of us have a deep-rooted resistance to acquiring a positive self-image and we have many subtle and obvious ways of sabotaging our attempts to change. We reject the attentions of the very people who could nurture and cherish us, dismissing their love and pushing them away in favour of those who criticise and misuse us. We plan to use daily affirmations to boost ourselves then mysteriously forget to do them. We resolve to clear up our clutter but somehow cannot quite bring ourselves to do it. We decide to start a creative project but suddenly we cannot be bothered, we lose interest. We decide to take some positive action, like exercise or joining a group then suddenly we cannot find the time to fit it in. We read all the right books but they make little difference. It is as if having self-esteem threatens our survival.

It is amazing how that saboteur can creep up, even when you thought it was gone. As I re-read this chapter to a friend I realised it had provoked the reactions I just described. While I sat writing, that old saboteur was busy scrambling my ability to understand what I was saying and I kept thinking "what a load of meaningless rubbish! Who's going to read this anyway?" And for a while I believed it; it wasn't until my friend said, "Your book makes perfect sense to me", that I realised what had been happening. The fact that it took me six months to start writing this chapter after having written several others, speaks for itself.

Any change to our identity, even a positive change, can feel threatening. Who will we become, how will we function, how will we cope, if we change? Even a destructive self-image is familiar, it is all we have known, and has in its own way kept us alive until now. We have developed all kinds of reference points and coping strategies around this identity of low self-esteem, if we change will any of them apply any more? We have got used to hiding ourselves behind dowdy clothes, behind food, behind drugs or alcohol. We have got used to deferring to others, to making do with the left-overs of life. We have become habituated to our own negativity, self-pity, frustration, resentment and blame. We have become attached to our fantasies of longing for love, for success, for the "someday my prince will come" syndrome.

If we agree to change, really agree, we will experience loss of all of this. It may sound crazy, but it still represents major loss. For some of us low self-esteem has served an important purpose, it has allowed us to hide and protect ourselves against exposure to criticism or attack. It has kept us invisible and isolated, but it has also kept us safe from having to stand up to those we fear, or whose power seems too great for us to challenge. It has helped us avoid taking responsibility for making changes, for breaking away from unhealthy relationships, work or surroundings.

We surround ourselves with people and activities that make our low self-image tolerable and indeed help to perpetuate it. If we were to mix with people who are confident and successful, it might only sharpen the contrast with our own state. I remember how I used to seek out others who also had problems with self-esteem, somehow I felt less uncomfortable with them. If I was with successful, confident people I felt worse about myself and envious of them, I would secretly try to find fault with them and their values, in order to feel better about myself. When I mixed with others who were lacking in confidence, they  understood me, I knew that they could tolerate my depression and sympathise to a degree that others would not. They, in turn, could offload their negativity on me and we would have long telephone conversations sharing our lot. Through listening to their problems and their inability to change things I could feel better about myself and my own state of stuckness. I am grateful because I know there are times that I could not have coped without that support, but there was also the element of collusion, of feeding each other's negativity. These friends did not challenge me; we had an investment in each other staying as we were.

It may be that low self-esteem is the family culture and confidence and assertion is seen as taboo. Perhaps being the one with low self-esteem is the habitual role we have played in our family or in our intimate relationship. If we change we would be breaking the family mould; if we change we may risk losing our relationships with those people who have an investment in us staying as we are.

It may mean that we finally have to leave the unsatisfactory job we are doing, because however poorly paid and however much it undermines our confidence it feels comfortable within our low self-esteem identity. It may mean that we will have to consider giving up the unhealthy lifestyle and habits we have used to comfort ourselves; smoking, drugs, alcohol. It might mean we will have to write that book we talked about writing for so long. Changing our sense of esteem can mean tackling all sorts of issues that we have put off and dealing with the consequences. So however we bitch and complain about having low self-esteem we can also have a big investment in staying put.

It is important to honour and respect our fears, and fearing change does not make us a pathetic wimp, it only makes us human. We need to understand what our investment is and how low self-esteem has served a purpose for us. We also need to decide whether or not we are ready to give it up. If it is very deep-rooted we will need to do it slowly, a step at a time, healing our fears one by one and replacing them with more positive ways of dealing with life.

Low self-esteem may have played an important part in our survival; for some of us the perception that we are bad is developed as a childhood defence against feelings of powerlessness and abandonment. We can experience abandonment for a variety of reasons: our parent was busy and did not come every time we cried or were hungry; we were separated from our parents at a young age in hospital, or at boarding school. Perhaps the separation was permanent through loss, divorce or adoption. Perhaps a parent was emotionally unavailable because they were caught up with their own needs, or their own dysfunction, or perhaps they were just not emotionally expressive. Abuse is also a form of abandonment, both on the part of the perpetrator and also those who failed to protect the child through disbelief and denial.

We can be abandoned emotionally as well as physically, either way it threatens our survival. Inside we experience the terror of the void, and a feeling that we do not exist. This is especially true if the abandonment is experienced before we had time to form a separate sense of our own identity, as described in the previous chapter. Furthermore we feel powerless in our abandonment, powerless to make others love and hold us. The emotional experience of abandonment is a painful combination of feeling powerless and alone; a combination most human beings will go to great lengths to avoid feeling. To a child, the idea of a parent, however negative, is preferable to no parent at all. No parent means total abandonment and rings a huge alarm bell to our instinctive mind, it tells us we will not survive.

We have to find ways to live with and to cope with the conflict between our need for a parent and the pain of what is happening to us. We convince ourselves that the abusive parent really meant well and we idealise them in order to protect ourselves against the knowledge that we are alone and the threat of total abandonment. We enter into a denial to defend against abandonment, but also to preserve our ability to love. It allows us to stay in touch with the idea and the experience of love and goodness, even if it is misdirected. This is how we begin to create the habit of idealising and romanticising relationships with people who misuse us.

Low self-esteem is another way in which we try to cope with this dilemma, and paradoxically it gives us a feeling of control over events. It eases that part of the pain of abandonment which is powerlessness. As children we tell ourselves it must be our fault that things go wrong, or that our parents don't love us the way we need them to. It must be because we are bad, or unlovable that they went away. In this way we give ourselves the illusion that we had control over their love for us and we have an outlet for our frustration and anger. We can take it out on ourselves and punish ourselves, because it is easier and safer than punishing others. If we were to express our anger we may justifiably fear their retaliation. Within our imagination, we may fear that our anger would destroy them. Somehow the notion that we were responsible is preferable to the reality that we were powerless to influence events or make people love us. In this way low self-esteem becomes a form of defence.

When as adults we attempt to heal those past wounds, ironically it is the recognition that we were powerless which helps to set us free. We were powerless over events and other people's behaviour, it was nothing to do with us at all. There is nothing we could have done, but now we are free, we can make choices for ourselves.

Sometimes the investment in low self-esteem points to deep conflicts about our existence. As one client P discovered, low self-esteem provided her with a hiding place, an excuse, and that it hid a deep ambivalence that went right to the core of her existence. It was buried so deep that she was unaware of what it was she was hiding. We were exploring her need for clutter and powerful resistance to discarding anything, and the image of her sitting in her pit of smoking or drinking and her desire to be invisible behind a wall of clutter. She talked about not wanting to be seen or spoken to. There was an underlying sense of inertia about it that pointed to something familiar.

Some people from the very beginning of their lives feel ambivalent about being here. By that I mean that they do not want to be alive in this physical world. They are often people who are psychically and spiritually sensitive, alive to inner realities. They may be highly empathetic and the outer world touches them very deeply. Perhaps they feel that they just do not fit and that life is too harsh and brutal to bear. The trouble is, it is too late, they are alive and this sets up ambivalence, a part of them that does not want to be here and a part of them that does.

One way of coping with this kind of existential ambivalence is to make a pact with yourself to resist engaging fully with life and then to forget about your decision and bury it deep in your unconscious. On the surface you pretend to be engaged, whilst passively resisting and going through the motions, the struggles of life. And believe me, if you are ambivalent about being here, life does tend to be a struggle. You yourself believe that you are trying, really trying, but something in you just keeps giving up, resisting, just will not budge and you are bewildered as to why, because you have forgotten. The energy just drains out of your efforts and there is an underlying pattern of inertia to all attempts to change. As a therapist I have encountered this kind of inertia and working with such an issue is hard work indeed. The person may have insights about their life problems, their negative thinking and self-destructive behaviour, but somewhere it all washes over them and nothing really changes. As the therapist you keep thinking the work is going somewhere and then it is as if it never happened.

Forgetting is an essential part of the strategy because if you knew and acknowledged how you felt, that part of you which does not want to be here would have to admit that it exists. As long as it remains hidden and invisible you can maintain the pretence of not really being here.

I imagine this all sounds complicated and convoluted to some of you, but those of you who recognise the dilemma will follow the threads. Perhaps it sounds a weird idea to pretend not to be alive in order to survive and on top of that to not even know you are doing it. However, it was also a part of my own journey and I was astounded to discover that hidden inert part of myself. Yet once I did, all kinds of things made sense, my inability to bring to fruition a lot of my talents and efforts.

Low self-esteem is a great cover, you get to fail, to be unwanted, invisible, it gives you a reason to give up trying. You can blame your childhood, traumatic events in your life, addiction to alcohol, smoking, depression or illness. But all this is a smoke screen that conceals the kind of deep-seated ambivalence I have described. It is a kind of spell with which we hypnotise ourselves and it powerfully binds our will into a state of passivity, a sense of paralysis and lack of commitment. We think we are committed to life when in fact we are not.

In order to change this we need to recognise that we have resistance and that we have an investment in continuing the way we are. We have to recognise and acknowledge our ambivalence to life and to honour with compassion our fears of being alive. The important thing is to uncover and recognise that question, Do I really want to be alive? To recognise the silent voice in us that does not want to admit to being alive. As I described earlier, the act of uncovering and acknowledging that hidden part of us that does not want to be here is an important step in breaking the spell. We also need to find a way of choosing to be here, to make a commitment to life. It seems simple to say this and in only a short paragraph, but the process can take time, weeks, or months in some cases. Living life once you have really chosen to be here is a whole lot easier than half living life while trying not to be. At least that's what I say to my clients when trying to encourage them that it is worthwhile.

The particular client P whom I mentioned earlier has found all sorts of behavioural changes arising spontaneously from acknowledging her ambivalence. She has begun to take initiatives at work, whereas previously she allowed herself to be overlooked and dismissed. She is beginning to find the energy to put into action some of the changes she previously only talked about. She is finding a kind of joy in her life that was hard to sustain before and she is discovering her will. It takes a lot of will to resist, the trouble is all the will is employed in saying "No" and there is none left for saying "Yes."

Resistance is an important survival strategy and we need to recognise its value. We need to be able to resist that which threatens our survival, or our integrity as individuals; we need to be able to say "No." However, the circumstances in which silent resistance, or inertia, was our only option, may no longer apply. As one client said, "I'm thirty-five and I make my own choices now!" In addition, we have acquired other experiences and resources that we can draw on. We need to recognise our resistance and seek to understand just how it has been trying to protect us. We may find that our resistance has now become self-destructive, but when we originally enlisted its support, it seemed the best option. Resistance is like a loyal soldier we set up to guard our psyche many moons ago then forgetting who gave them their instructions we now blame them for getting in our way.

I often tell the story of the instances of individual Japanese soldiers who survived alone on remote tiny islands in the Pacific up to twenty years after the Second World War. Soldiers who were sole survivors of their platoons, but who loyally continued to perform their duties. They would raise the flag, patrol the island day after day. It seems bizarre to imagine such loyalty and hard to imagine what it might be like on that day when a boat finally appeared and they were told that the War was over. Not only were they told that the War was over, but that it had been over many years ago. I ask my clients to try to imagine what it would be like to return to a country that had changed utterly, to a society and to a family of people no longer recognisable. What would it be like to adjust to such a change? I tell them that the Japanese value loyalty and that those soldiers were not laughed at, but were rewarded with medals for their sense of duty and then retired very, very gently.

The story is a strange and memorable one, and yet each of us has one of those loyal soldiers inside us. If we just try to get rid of them they will resist, because that is their nature and that is what we told them to do. The way to deal with them is to understand just how they have been trying to serve us and to thank them for their efforts. Then gently but firmly, we have to let them know that the War is over, that we are now in charge and that their duties have now changed.

Activities

How do you resist self-esteem?

❖ What is your particular style of resistance? Do you ignore or negate compliments others try to give you? Do you dress in black shabby clothes that hide you? Do you seek friends who you don't really like because you think that is what you deserve? Do you apply for jobs that are beneath your capability? Do you mysteriously forget to do good things for yourself, or make sure you don't have the time? Do you live in a mess and find it impossible to clear a space for yourself?

Has low self-esteem served a purpose for you?

❖ See if you can discover your investments in hanging onto low self-esteem.
❖ What are your fears of changing into someone who has self-worth?
❖ Include other people's investment in keeping you as you are, how do others try to keep you down?

Acknowledging your fears and resistances.

❖ Imagine speaking to them as if they were loyal soldiers and see if you can appreciate that they have been trying to protect you in their own peculiar way.

❖ Let them know that they have done their job and that you now have the opportunity to make new choices and that you will be learning new ways together.

❖ Ask them if they are willing to learn with you.

Reward Yourself

Well done! Give yourself a really BIG strawberry or three for having the courage to admit your resistance! DO something that really makes you feel good, go out to the pictures, put your feet up, phone a friend, buy yourself a present. Even if you didn't manage to admit your resistance but still read the chapter, forgive yourself and reward yourself anyway, it's a good habit to encourage!

3

The Shame Factor

Low self-esteem can trigger a number of different emotions; anger, fear, anxiety, depression or guilt, but one of the commonest underlying feelings is that of shame. Shame is a feeling that goes beyond what we have done or not done, it is the belief and feeling that who we are is bad. We want to hide ourselves away and not let anyone see or get close to us. When we feel shame we feel tainted, dirty, that we deserve to be punished, even perhaps that we do not deserve to be alive. Above all we must not let anyone know our shame; it must be kept secret at all costs. We will try to bury and hide our shame even from ourselves. It is a painful experience that can lead to self-destructive behaviour such as self-harm, abuse of alcohol, drugs, food, anything to numb the feeling.

Shame touches the very core of our sense of self, it concerns our spiritual relationship with life, our connection to the Whole and to God. This is why shame and guilt can be associated with religious beliefs and there are religious belief systems which encourage the notion that we are fundamentally bad or sinful. This can create a powerful culture of shame.

The Adam and Eve story is a very vivid description of what it is like to experience shame. There is a sense of shocking exposure, a sense of our own nakedness and the urge to hide. We fear the rejection and disapproval of those closest to us. When we feel shame we banish ourselves from the Garden of Eden, we close our heart to ourselves. We exist in exile in the belief that we can never return.

The author John Bradshaw ("Healing the Shame that Binds You") differentiates between what he calls "healthy shame" and "toxic shame". According to Bradshaw, "healthy shame" is the appropriate recognition of our human limitations, that we are not omnipotent. When we act against our own integrity we experience a prod from our conscience. It shows us when we have overstepped the mark, broken our moral code. It may be experienced as embarrassment and probably will include some sense of remorse. Toxic shame on the other hand, disables us and is usually an intense overreaction to the circumstances which trigger it

There are people who lack shame, who behave without respect for others or themselves and who appear to be untroubled by their actions. Shameless behaviour might be due to a lack of awareness or ignorance; it can also be deliberate. An extreme example of a person who is shameless would be called a psychopath and this condition is described as a personality disorder.

As children we sometimes learn to carry shame for adults around us, when they are unaware or unwilling to take responsibility for their actions. We develop the habit of apologising for their behaviour as if it were our own. Children of addicts and alcoholics may be familiar with this tendency.

According to Bradshaw, toxic shame is invariably imposed on us by others. It is created through the overt and the subtle messages we received in childhood and took into our psyche, believing them to be true. In other words, another shamed us into believing that we were bad. One common example is being told that we are a bad girl/boy when we misbehaved. Healthy parenting distinguishes between a child's actions and who they are, affirming the child is still loved, while challenging their behaviour. Children so easily believe they are bad when being told off. Being consistently given the message that we are bad invariably leads to chronic low self-esteem.

Name-calling is a way of shaming someone, often in connection to their appearance, their background, race, or intelligence. That is why name-calling is a common feature of bullying. We know it hurts, and that labels stick. Sometimes shame evolves through neglect. If we have experienced neglect, physically, emotionally, or mentally, we may conclude that it must be because we were bad and deserved to be abandoned.

Shame is a strong component of abuse in all its forms. People who suffer abuse often feel a sense of shame, that they must have done something to deserve it. This feeling of shame can be quite crippling and a major factor in preventing the sufferer from taking action. It is the weapon most frequently used by perpetrators to undermine and to gain a hold over the person they are abusing. Abusers tell their victims that they deserve it, that they are responsible for the abuse. Abuse is a way of passing on unwanted shame to someone else, an attempt on the part of the perpetrator to expel their disowned shame.

Pia Mellody, another author and pioneer in the field of addiction recovery work, talks about shame binds. These are the areas of our lives which hold and trigger shame. We might have a shame bind about our body image, or our intelligence with the belief that we are stupid.

Areas That Trigger Shame

❖ Body Image - shame about size, attractiveness; the belief that we are ugly, too fat, tall, small; being shamed for physical difference through race or distinctive features.

❖ Intelligence - the fear that we are stupid; shame about illiteracy, dyslexia. It is possible to feel shame for being too clever. This can also connect with shame about success and failure.

❖ Emotional Neediness - we may feel needy and ashamed of making demands, we may also feel ashamed of being uncontrolled in our neediness.

❖ Expressing Emotions - we may have shame binds around expressing emotions such as anger or vulnerability. It can also be triggered by others expressing emotions towards us, such as anger. It can even be linked to speaking out, to making a sound.

❖ Being Selfish - the fear that being selfish, or being seen to be so, is shameful.

❖ Sexuality - a major source of shame, not only as a result of individual experience but also through messages widely held by society and religious beliefs. Shame about sexual orientation; bodily shame connected with sexuality.

We will react in any situation that reminds us of that shamed sense of ourselves. The slightest reminder can trigger us. Some people become angry and blaming towards others who say something that reminds the person of their bad self. It is imperative that the shame be kept hidden. This can be very confusing for the onlooker who experiences being accused of actions that are quite alien to them. Sometimes they are on the receiving end of the very actions they are being accused of. This kind of aggressive defensiveness is called projection and is very difficult to deal with.

If we are out of touch with our shame, if it is hidden from our awareness, a good clue is to look for the places where we tend to blame others. If we turn around the blame finger and point it towards ourselves, there is a good probability that shame will be lurking around somewhere close by.

We might be oversensitive to criticism, or imagine we are being criticised when we are not and then feel overwhelmed with guilt. We will have a horror of upsetting others, or hurting their feelings. We feel inappropriately responsible for another's feelings and automatically blame ourselves for any conflict or upset. As this triggers our shame we tumble into a desperate need to make things better, to placate the other and lose all sense of proportion about our part in the situation. In shame situations we feel very exposed and believe, "if they really knew me they wouldn't want to". A common reaction is to withdraw and close down all communication.

An intense shame reaction has been called a shame attack. It is not unlike a panic attack in that the symptoms are quite overwhelming and immobilising. At first we become disorientated and numb, finding it hard to collect our thoughts or even to form words; we feel frozen. This then turns to distress, depression, self-hate and fear of contact with others. We can obsess continually, going over events again and again in a desperate attempt to rid ourselves of shame. "If only we'd done this, if only we hadn't done that." Shame attacks can be brief lasting only a couple of minutes; they can also last for days before we feel recovered enough to face the world again.

When We Break The Denial- We Break The Spell!

The first key to dealing with toxic shame is finding a way to break the denial. Shame thrives on secrecy and denial. Acknowledging and owning our shame to ourselves is the first step, disowned shame creates lies and manipulation; it begets violence and destruction, to ourselves and to others. The next step is finding the courage to talk about it to someone else. This begins to break the hold it has over us. In our own minds the content of our shame seems utterly impossible, unforgivable. As we find the courage to communicate our shame we often find we have exaggerated its significance. We are so hard on ourselves. This sense of over-exaggeration is typical of toxic shame. We need to re-define our sense of proportion. Was our action really so dreadful? We have the right to make mistakes, to not be perfect. We need to become more forgiving to ourselves.

When we have a pattern of feeling shame, we find it hard to know what is a healthy degree of responsibility and what is not. We find it hard to know how much responsibility lies with us and how much lies with others. Talking to someone else gives us a valuable reference point, a reality check. Others will often give immediate responses that say, "It really isn't that bad" and "that had nothing to do with you; that's their responsibility!"

We need to find a sense of discrimination, in other words, how much of the shame is ours and how much belongs to someone else? Maybe we do not need to carry it, maybe we can let it go. The act of realising and affirming to ourselves that the shame we carry does not belong to us can be very liberating. It allows us to feel our anger and reclaim our sense of power and respect. Finding creative ways to symbolically hand back the shame to where it belongs is helpful.

Sometimes when we discover the shame we have carried belongs to another we need to express our anger at having been shamed. Unexpressed anger and rage can cause all kinds of problems; it tends to seep out or explode on those close to us, or backfires on us in all kinds of destructive ways. Communicating our anger is the most important means of expression, but sometimes it is not appropriate. There are several well-known techniques used to express strong anger or rage. Some methods involve releasing physical aggression in a controlled setting such as punching cushions, hitting the mattress, smashing objects. Vigorous sports or activities such as gardening can also be a way of releasing aggression. The important point is to ensure that the activity is safe in that you will not harm another or yourself. Writing unsent letters is another commonly used method. You can express in an uncensored way all that you feel, and you can keep working on and refining the letter until you feel satisfied. You may or may not decide to send the letter; if not, then you need to decide how you are going to dispose of it. A ritual burning or tearing- up of the letter can be satisfying.

Anger holds enormous energy which can be transformed into positive action and creativity. I recently found myself in a situation where my rage was triggered towards myself. Not having done this for some time, I was astounded at the viciousness with which I was tearing into myself. There was a loose bit of wallpaper on the landing and I pulled it off a bit more each time I went upstairs. I had planned to decorate anyway and so I thought now might be a good time to start. I directed the energy of obsessing with anger, into stripping the hall, stairs and landing. Tearing at the wallpaper instead of myself alleviated my anger and I became absorbed in the task, not a task I relish under normal circumstances I can tell you. In three days I had stripped the entire hall, stairs and landing; a) I got the job done without effort and b) I tore at the walls instead of myself. However, it was sobering to look at the physical space and the amount of anger it represented.

We can also work with anger and shame through the use of spiritual practice and consciousness. Meditation can be used to develop the ability to witness our feelings and penetrate layer by layer to the source of their hold on our psyche. Working step by step towards forgiveness is a path of healing. We can recognise that holding onto shame or resentment only serves to keep us locked and imprisoned in the pain of the past, and that we are the ones who end up eating away at ourselves and prolonging the hurt. In addition it keeps us tied and connected to those who hurt us and we drag them around forever in our psyche instead of leaving them behind. Forgiveness does not deny what happened, but it frees us and allows us to move on. As the author Dr Jerry Jamploski put it "Do you want to be right or do you want to be free?" And this is the choice; which is more important to us, continually re-running a hurt and resentful past that has gone, or letting go and moving into a future that is ours?

Activities

Find a way of symbolically handing back the shame to the person to whom it belongs.

❖ Write an unsent letter. Not sending the letter gives you freedom to vent your feelings in an uncensored way and without fear of retaliation, just write as you feel. Handwriting the letter allows you to press into the paper with your pen, whilst using a word processor can give you a feeling of control and precision. If you wish you can later send an edited version of your letter to the person concerned. Many people find this simple exercise both powerful and releasing. You may wish to destroy your letter afterwards, by tearing and burning it.
❖ Find or create an object that represents your shame; it may be a stone or a clay object, or a doll. Making the object allows you to connect to different feelings and aspects of your shame. When you feel ready, find a ritual way of releasing the object by burying it, burning it or releasing it into water.

Healing Visualisation for Shame

Using our imagination and visualisation is a powerful way to access parts of us beyond our rational mind. It provides an arena for us to interact with our inner world and we can use images to heal and transform our experience. Whether or not we see vivid images and colours is irrelevant; we all have fantasies and it is this capacity we are tapping into. In this particular visualisation we use the healing qualities of water and light to cleanse and the wise being as a symbol of our own higher self to transform our hurt. When visualising it is important to create a quiet environment where you will not be interrupted by telephones or other people. You can lie or sit, whatever feels most comfortable. Try and think of this as a strawberry, time to relax and treat yourself to the healing powers of your own imagination. If you wish you can record the instructions so you can just lie back and listen to it without worrying what comes next. Remember to leave space for yourself to complete the actions.

❖ Imagine yourself in a special place in the landscape, a place that feels peaceful. There is a pool of water there and in the centre of the pool is a fountain.
❖ Waiting by the pool is a wise spiritual being who is unconditionally loving towards you.
❖ Offer them your shame for transformation. You may see your shame in symbolic form as a dark cloud, or an ashtray full of dog-ends, for example.
❖ Whatever form your shame takes, let it be released into forgiveness and redemption
❖ Ask that your innocence be returned
❖ Feel the radiance of love that flows from your Sacred Power.
❖ Let it touch you, enter you, cleanse you
❖ Bathe in the Pool of Redemption, float in its healing waters.
❖ Swim towards the centre to the Fountain of Innocence. Play in its dancing sparkling water, let the rainbow droplets remind you of your natural innocence.
❖ Let the radiant sun of their presence warm and dry your dank secret places.

❖ Let the light of love stream into your denied self, sparking a seed of openess that begins to spread through your body and being.

Know that who you are is loved, is known
You are a daughter of the soft earth, a son of the red rock
Unto you is returned your natural self
For you are part of Creation always and everywhere

Reward Yourself

Reward yourself especially after reading this chapter. You deserve to be kind to yourself, curl up and comfort yourself in some way if this chapter has stirred up painful experiences for you. Listen to some soothing music, or watch a movie, but please don't punish yourself!

4

Addiction to Longing
and The Wounded Dream

"I now have lots of strategies for looking at myself and relationships in a new light, I don't expect so much of myself or beat myself up for being weak. I'm a lot calmer and a lot less defensive."

Relationships are possibly the most sensitive and complex area affected by low self-esteem. The ability to create and sustain healthy relationships is a deep issue for so many of us. Having a partner, marriage, and having a family remain the expectations of society. This is despite the fact that relationships increasingly break down and that serial monogamy is becoming more and more the trend. Our expectation of relationships, that they be based on love and good sex is a modern notion, at least in Western society. Marriage has for centuries been a social contract, a practical institution, rather than a romantic one. Breaking the traditions of duty and commitment to family has freed up our desires and our longings. It has liberated people, especially women, from being condemned to miserable life- sentences. And who can dismiss the right of someone to be freed from abuse, from slavery and enforced misery? The sexual revolution has brought all sorts of choices about what type of relationship we choose, including same sex relationships.

Having said this, we cannot shrug off thousands of years of history in just a few decades, the old conditioning lies deep within our psyche. With our choices have come new responsibilities and consequences. These changes have cost us in stability and connection to extended family, and the arguments against such liberation are still voiced in cultures other than our own. Whilst sexually transmitted diseases have always been a part of life, we are far more exposed to these dangers. Above all it has raised our expectations, perhaps to an impossible degree, of what we want from a relationship: lover, soul mate, companion, freedom, provider, co-parent. Consequently it also impacts on what we expect of ourselves. In the past, our courting days were restricted to a few brief teenage years and then they were over unless we were prematurely widowed. Now we have to keep looking, to keep putting it out in search of a partner, throughout our lives. We experience more frequently the pain and loss of relationship.

Self-esteem affects our relationships in all sorts of ways: our body image and confidence in our desirability, our confidence in addressing our needs and getting them met with another person, our ability to trust and to cope with intimacy. It also affects our ability to assert ourselves and to draw clear boundaries, as well as our communication skills and ability to deal with conflict.

We can react by avoiding relationships altogether, avoiding close contact with anyone who would discover just how awful we are. "Besides", we tell ourselves, "Who'd find me attractive?" Low self-esteem can stop us from socialising, from having the courage to chat someone up. We may unconsciously choose partners who are not available, or we leave when things get too secure, telling ourselves it was "them not us!"

Lack of self-worth can also cause us to seek and to stay with partners who undermine and abuse us, or who simply do not value us. We choose partners who we do not really respect or value because we believe this is all we deserve. When we are unable to value ourselves, when we are desperate for love or to feel wanted, we will give ourselves sexually to anyone who appears to want us. We feel flattered by anyone who gives us attention and blind ourselves to whether or not they have our best interests at heart. We also do these things because it is what is familiar and what is safe; sadly we are habituated into being used or neglected, to expecting only a few crumbs.

When we have low self-esteem we tell ourselves that it is our fault our relationships fail, regardless of the crummy behaviour of our partners. We use each experience to hammer another nail into our failed relationship coffin. We believe,

"There must be something terribly wrong with me, I'm ugly, I'm too needy, I'm unlovable". God forbid it should be their lack of consideration, their bullying, or their selfish behaviour.

In the same way that we prefer to hang out with others who have low self-esteem because it is less threatening, less exposing, so we also settle for less in our primary relationships. To be exposed to anything more would feel not only unfamiliar and alien, but also too painful. Ironically some of us with low self-esteem can find it too hard to cope with a loving, supportive relationship, because it puts us in touch with the losses of our past and poses too great a challenge to the lack of love we feel for ourselves. In this situation we will try very hard to sabotage the love our partner feels for us. Being in relationship with someone who has chronic low self esteem is very difficult when they disbelieve and reject your protestations of love, when they try to push you away, or are dogged by the constant and unfounded insecurity that you will leave them for someone else. You find your love is continually blocked and whatever you do, you are powerless to convince them that they are loved.

We are affected by our childhood experience, how we experienced the relationship of our parents and other adults around, including lack of relationship. Our relationship to our parents, or parent figures, has perhaps the most profound impact of all upon our psyche. Some of us do manage to create the kind

At last someone who'll look after me!.

of nurturing and satisfying relationship that we want, and sometimes in stark contrast to our childhood experience. I have met people whose experience of abandonment and abuse has determined and enabled them to create the opposite, a safe and loving partnership.

Despite our desires or intention, sadly we often end up recreating the same kind of relationship we had with a particular parent or mixture of both. If we had a parent or parents who were unavailable or critical, then we may find ourselves, despite our best efforts, in relationship with partners who do the same. If we were the carers of dependent, or needy parents, we may find partners who at first appear strong and caring, then inexplicably and suddenly they have crises which force us into the carer role, pushing our own needs aside. The reasons for this are complex, there is no one answer and it would be simplistic of me to suggest this. However, I have found some clues along the way.

We could say that the psychological function of parents is to reflect and to encourage a positive, nurturing and capable image to their children. We gradually learn to take this into ourselves, to internalise it, until it becomes our self-image. We instinctively know what we need and if we do not get it we will continue to seek and to strive in all sorts of ways until we fulfil these developmental needs, the missing pieces of our personality jigsaw, until we have completed the task. We could call this a drive towards wholeness and it is an extremely strong drive, a survival instinct. Roberto Assagioli, the founder of Psychosynthesis, recognised this as a fundamental evolutionary drive. This is why he preferred the term Psychosynthesis (a coming together of parts to form a whole), rather than the term Psychoanalysis (a breaking down into bits), used by his contemporary Sigmund Freud in describing the therapeutic journey. However we describe it, the drive is strong and no matter how many times we fail, or are obstructed, we will keep on until we get there.

Addiction to Longing and the Wounded Dream

This is a term I use to describe a particular pattern sometimes found amongst people with low self-esteem. I spoke in chapter two about the way we convince ourselves it is our fault that we are not loved or cared for, in order to regain a feeling of control and as a safe outlet for our anger. I also spoke about how we idealise our parents or our situation in order to protect ourselves from the painful reality and in order to keep love alive in our hearts. Our need to love is as strong as our need to be loved. If the subject of our love is rejecting or absent, then we can idealise them to compensate. We enter into a denial of the wounded reality and cling onto a romanticised version of our situation and of the people involved. It is this tendency to idealise which I want to explore here and how it affects our perception and experience of relationships.

The other aspect is to do with our evolutionary need to complete the missing pieces of the jigsaw of our psyche. We retain a dream of the things that we needed and didn't get as a child. We then seek for and project this fantasy onto our relationships. We fall in love with the idealised dream. The trouble is that the dream masks a wounded reality which is what we invariably end up with. Another way of describing this is that we try to get someone else to fill our childhood gap, to give us all the things our parents did not give us as children. What we invariably end up with is a partner who recreates the hurts of the past and who is horribly like the parent we didn't want e.g. "the one who will finally give me the approval I need", turns into a critical partner. "The one who will be there for me", turns into the partner who is abandoning, rejecting or too needy themselves to support us.

The longing for our potential wholeness, for our dream, is incredibly deep and strong. We delude ourselves into believing that a lousy relationship will eventually work out, because we are convinced of its potential. All relationships have potential, but potentials are just that, there is no guarantee that they will become reality. In this case the potential is based on a fantasy that was not and therefore cannot be realised; it is too late, our childhood is over and now we have to sink or swim as adults. Our job is to find a partner, not a surrogate parent; so the dream has to betray us.

Some of us cling steadfastly to our dream to a masochistic degree, defying and denying an abusive reality. We put up with a destructive relationship long after others would have left, and our friends do leave, unable to continue watching us suffer. We cling to our dream of potential in a relationship, unable and unwilling to recognise or acknowledge that it is unworkable. It seems that in these cases we have an inability to distinguish between a realistic potential and a fantasy one.

Even if we do recognise its destructiveness, we still keep on clinging to hope, to forgiveness, convincing ourselves that we are being compassionate and loving instead of the reality that we are allowing ourselves to be humiliated and mistreated. And even if we recognise all of this, that we are caught in a destructive pattern and that we are deluding ourselves, we can still feel powerless to break it. It is so hard to shake off that dream.

In some ways our refusal to give up on our dream could be seen as admirable, as a determination not to give up on ourselves. I know I have myself believed that to let go of the dream would mean giving up on myself. However, in the kind of situations I have described, that determination is misplaced and ultimately, terribly destructive.

Longing has qualities of intensity, passion and joy. It carries the hope of fulfilment. Longing is a great motivator, a carrot that keeps us hooked. Longing has its place in the spiritual journey with a vision of God, of unity, of Nirvana, that keeps us seeking the truth. And so longing drives our need for love, and keeps its flame alive. It serves another purpose in enabling us to keep reality at bay. While we can do this we do not have to deal with the situation, to face our fears, or our shortcomings. We can stay safely in a state of longing.

Longing is a kind of fix; when we cannot experience fulfilment we can alleviate our frustration with fantasies of longing. If, as children we were denied love, we may have learned to experience longing as the next best thing, the nearest substitute. Longing has a craving, addictive quality to it and it can become a habit. We fall in longing with people who are unavailable; people who live far away, who are involved with someone else, or who are detached, rejecting, or aloof in their personality. This creates anguish, but the distance allows us to cling onto the possibility that some day they will give us what we need. It allows us to perpetuate our fantasy and avoid having to confront giving up hope.

The writer Pia Mellody deals with this kind of destructive relationship cycle in her book "Facing Love Addiction". It is a masterly work on the patterns of addictive and destructive relating. She has her own way of defining these patterns and writes about the love addict and the avoidance addict and how we are either identified with one or the other, or swap about in tortuous duos. The love addict is terrified of abandonment and will cling, demand and threaten suicide to hang onto relationship. The avoidance addict is terrified of being trapped and is aloof, distant and maintains a sense of control by avoiding closeness.

Unfortunately those of us who have these issues get caught in repeated cycles of similar relationships. Each time we swear to ourselves that we will do it differently next time, but despite our best intentions and despite appearances to the contrary, we find ourselves in variations of the same painful dynamics again and again. Each time our self-esteem is knocked down yet again and we lose more of our confidence to form a healthy relationship.

Breaking the Spell

I do not pretend to know all the answers but it seems to me that one of our major tasks is to wake up from our dream, to face the painful reality and the past that engendered it. We need to come to terms with the fact that we will never replace that childhood time of being cared for and loved in the way we needed. We have to mourn the loss of what we never had. When we are children, we have a right to expect others to take care of our needs but that time is over and now we are adults, we can no longer expect another to do it for us in that way. We have to find a way to learn how to give it to ourselves.

At this point I would like to give a portrait of someone's experience of her addiction to longing. J was born in this country then at the age of three she and her family moved to New Zealand. Her father became a sheep farmer and they lived in the countryside. She describes an idyllic life of freedom and adventure, of being with her father on horseback and exploring together. She describes herself as confident and adventurous, unafraid of the dark, the wild. At the age of eleven she, her brothers and her mother went on what she thought was a holiday. They returned to England by boat. In fact her mother had left her father, to live with a man who she had never met. She virtually never saw her father again until she was in her thirties.

Her new situation was in bleak contrast and very unhappy. J clung to dreams of her childhood past with her father and perceived him as the wronged one. She blamed herself for the fact that he did not contact her and lost all her confidence and became fearful.

When I met her she was involved with a Frenchman with whom she had had children. The relationship had struggled for years, exacerbated by her husband's problems recovering from alcohol addiction and chronic ill health. Also he had difficulty in controlling his anger. For a long time they lived apart but maintained the relationship, he remained in France and she in England. The situation dragged on for years, as she clung to her faith in the potential of the relationship and in her compassion for him. She was unable to make the final break, for fear of doing to her children what had happened to her.

We looked at the different themes that were keeping her in this relationship and saw their connections with her early life. We revisited her idyllic childhood and acknowledged the pain. She grieved for the loss of her father and her natural confidence. We began to question the reality that he had made no real effort to maintain contact with her. What also emerged was the fact that he had problems with alcohol, something she had chosen to gloss over. She realised how she had made excuses for him and chosen to ignore things to preserve her dream. By allowing a more balanced picture of the past, she was able to admit and express feelings of anger towards her father. She made contact with him and eventually they were able to establish a more real relationship and acknowledge some of the hurts of the past.

In facing the truth about her relationships with her husband and with her father, she was finally able to resolve this situation. J saw how she had transferred her idealisation of her father onto her fantasy of potential in her relationship. She recognised that she was recreating her mother's belief that if only she had stuck it out everything would have been alright. She realised she was projecting her own needs onto her children and that their experience was different from hers. She let go and soon met another partner and was able to establish a very different kind of relationship, one that empowered and supported her.

Waking up from our wounded dream does not happen overnight. It is a process that takes time, months or even years, as the threads and layers of our dream and our attachment to it, are revealed. For some of us, each relationship provides a clue, a piece of the dream we are unconsciously holding. For others it takes prolonged periods of counselling or psychotherapy to unearth and break the dream. Reading books such as this one, and gathering information that we can identify with can help us to become aware of what we are doing. Whatever the case, the intention to start is the most important part of the journey.

It takes Two

One of the facts we need to consider is that there are two people in this situation, for we are often attracted to people who are also suffering from low self-esteem. In other words we often tend to have relationships with people who have their own version of the same issues. Facing Love Addiction describes in detail one of the classic dynamics of dysfunctional relationships. As I mentioned earlier, one partner tends to be clingy, needy, demanding and the other aloof, distant and independent. My own experience is that I can alternate, in one relationship I'm the needy one and in the next I find I'm the unavailable, rejecting one.

So what happens if two people with low self-esteem form a relationship with each other? They may find solace in each other, comfort and understand each other. However, if they are both banking on the hope that the other will make up for that childhood gap, then it gets complicated. We could call such relationships 'replacementships'. In a replacementship we try to get others fill the hole inside us. This kind of dependency has to end in frustration, because neither party has what it takes to give to the other; both are too emotionally hungry. Besides, they cannot do it for us, because it is not their job. What sometimes happens is that each party feels let down, abandoned and frustrated by the other. When we feel let down, it presses into the wounds of our childhood and we feel stuck with how to resolve the hurt, anger and frustration of our unfulfilled need.

What can then happen is that our partner becomes the target for our pent up rage and frustration. There may be current issues within the relationship which act as triggers. But the bulk of the feelings are from our past which are then unleashed, quite unfairly, onto our nearest and dearest. When we overlay a past relationship with a parent figure onto another person, this is called transference. We confuse our past relationship with our present one and project our feelings from the past onto the present. This pattern of overreaction can be devastating as both partners struggle to understand and contain the dynamic.

I am not suggesting that so called healthy relationships are devoid of these issues. There are elements of child/parent dynamic in many relationships. However, if the relationship is primarily based on and dominated by these dynamics, then it becomes much more intense.

Some people become rescuers, trying to fix other people's pain. We enjoy taking care of others, because it makes us feel better about ourselves, it alleviates our low self-esteem. We then attract and are attracted to people who are needy or in trouble. It makes us feel needed, important and takes the attention away from our own issues. When things go wrong in the relationship, we can blame it on their neediness, their drinking, their problems. We may habitually put them first at the expense of ourselves then can end up feeling drained, unsupported and resentful. This is a tricky issue for how can we tell when being caring and loving stops being a virtue and starts to be a dysfunction? For many of us it is safer to give than receive; giving ensures that we stay in control, receiving means accepting that we are good enough to be loved.

How do we change all this? How do we get to a place where we can feel fulfilled and nurtured by our relationships? I am sure many of you will have your own answers to these questions, and with each relationship we learn a little more about ourselves and about relating. Each relationship has its own gift and each person we relate to teaches us something new about how to be.

At the end of the day we have to find the answers in ourselves. We have to find the strength, courage and compassion to create self-worth in ourselves when we've never learned how.

We have to learn how to create it from scratch and grow it into a natural state of being. We have to start to learn how to create those things for ourselves and stop expecting others to do it for us. Their approval, their need of us will not give us self worth, it will only give us a fix and will keep us in a state of dependency. Our dependency on others for making us feel worthy is at very best unreliable, and at its worst it is life threatening.

We have to face and mourn the loss of our childhood disappointments and deprivation. We have to find a way to honour and let go of our anger and disappointment and stop blaming. We have to overcome the terror of our feelings of abandonment and learn to cherish our own company. We have to discover that we are strong enough to stand on our own two feet and that we are capable. We have to recognise that our opinions and feelings matter and that if we respect ourselves, we will make sure that others treat us with the same respect. We have to learn that it is ok to have needs and to discover what we can and what we cannot realistically expect from another.

We have to accept that relationships succeed and fail for all kinds of reasons, that it might be nobody's fault and not necessarily ours if someone rejects us. Those of us with low self-esteem often have it wired up as, "Other people know how to have relationships, other people don't get rejected, everyone else has someone but me!" By the end of this book, or at least through the next couple of chapters, I hope that you will learn how to stop punishing yourself and how to safeguard your feelings of self-worth at times when you are hurt or rejected. We have to discover that we are after all loveable, that we do matter to ourself and consequently to others.

When we are able to accept and stand up for our own lovability, paradoxically we start to attract and be attracted to others who do cherish and respect us. At least, we become much less tolerant of hanging around those who do not treat us well and are quicker to recognise and respond when it does happen.

Activities

What is your dream?

❖ Is there an unfulfilled dream that you carry from your childhood? Can you write it down as if it were a fairy story? "Once upon a time there was a little girl/boy who........"

❖ See if you can explore how you project this dream onto your current relationships and what happens, or has happened when you do?

Releasing The Dream

❖ If you feel at a point when you are ready to let go of your childhood dream then you can find creative ways to do this. Create a symbol of your unfulfilled longing and ritually bury it, burn it or cast it onto water. You can use visualisation to hand it over to a wise being, or to Life to take care of it.

❖ You can affirm your intention to let go of your old dream by repeating phrases such as, "I am now meeting my own needs, I am my own parent".

I do not want to be too prescriptive at this point because the way we need to come to terms, grieve and finally relinquish our broken dreams is such an individual task and one that often emerges spontaneously. I trust that working through this book as a whole, will contribute towards the healing of your broken dream.

Reward Yourself

This chapter has probably brought up many feelings for you and instead of punishing yourself, as is your usual habit, be kind and gentle with yourself. It takes time to heal these matters and sometimes a lifetime. So give yourself a strawberry, stroke a cat, go for a walk, cuddle up under a duvet, or dance your anger out with some wild music.

5

Breaking The Spell

"I'm a changed person. All those years of abusing myself, it took less than a week and one simple thing. I felt so strong standing up for myself against that inner voice that always put me down. Now the voice has gone!"

New Year Resolution

Sniff the track, catch the scent
poke snout out of burrow into sharp frosty air
as the echoes of the last departing guest subside
and in the quiet of these first days
I wonder where the wind'll blow me

letting go, learning to disentangle
are the seeds my soul picked out for me to cultivate?
from this new century's catalogue.

Sinking snout into wet leaf mould
of the little earthy track
I determine to follow through hazel thickets
to Vobster and beyond
savouring the new sensation
of departing from obsess and possess
and other mindfields of intensity.

Leaving the self-accuser at the crossroads
her baggage of blame now redundant about her feet

her sharp fingernose will gather dewdrops instead
and me no longer there for her to point at

If we could learn to leave our hate at this threshold
if we could do this what a pile there'd be
what a World!

The Moment We Recognise Self-Criticism Is A Form Of Abuse And That It Has To Stop - We Break The Spell!

People with low self-esteem often believe they have to improve themselves in order to gain self-esteem, they are continually working on and driving themselves to endless self-improvement. In fact what is needed is to stop the attitudes and behaviours that maintain self-hate. Ironically these are often the very attitudes and behaviours that we are using in order to achieve the esteem we so desperately long for. It is astonishing, just how much effort goes into maintaining low self-esteem, on a day to day basis. We punish and undermine ourselves incessantly with such thoughts as; "Typical! Stupid! Pathetic! You're bad, why can't you do it properly? It's just not good enough, you should...." the variations run on forever. The phrases are often casual and may in themselves seem harmless but, as we discovered when we started examining our language for sexism and racism, words are potent. In effect we brainwash ourselves on a daily basis and the methods we use to try and achieve self-worth are the very means that keep us in worthlessness.

We become adept at preventing ourselves from changing or from gaining any sense of satisfaction with thoughts like; "What's the point? You'll never do it, you never get it right, you should have done it differently, you always get it wrong."

Year after year, day after day, those words take on enormous power, they overwhelm us and they crush us and we believe we are powerless in the face of them. It is as if we were held in a spell. We long for the day when we will finally feel good enough about ourselves and then we will have self-esteem. We forget who it is that gives those negative thoughts credence and power in the first place.

We may believe we need to heal the past, to go back over our histories of wounds and hurts, to express our anger, our abandonment and feelings of rejection. We may feel we need to understand and forgive ourselves and those who imprinted us with messages of worthlessness. Then perhaps, we will feel better about ourselves. This is an important part of the journey, to allow ourselves to feel the betrayal, the anger, the grief; but does it change how we operate now?

For myself it was not enough. I spent years digging away at a dysfunctional past, but it was not enough to change my sense of lovability, my inner confidence or to stop the terrifying months of despair and depression. Despite being a therapist and deeply valuing the work, I have sometimes wondered if long-term therapy is counterproductive in that it subtly colludes with the belief that there is something wrong with us. In other words that we have to keep working at improving ourselves until we finally get sorted out enough to acquire self-esteem. It wasn't until I finally recognised what I was doing to myself and that it had to stop, that things really began to change.

Whatever our story, whatever the cruelty or neglect we have endured, however long that story, I say it is right now, each day, that we ourselves perpetuate the beliefs and the suffering of chronic low self-esteem. The point being, regardless of the past, what can we do now to change our thoughts and behaviour so we can move forward with dignity, love and respect?

At a certain point in my life, when my self-worth and confidence had been shattered, I went on a meditation retreat at a Buddhist Centre. The approach is called Insight Meditation and is based on the Vipassana Meditation techniques practised through S E Asia. We were taught to simply focus on our breathing and to observe the thoughts that inevitably distract us. The aim is to begin to detach from thoughts and to loosen the belief that our thoughts are our identity. One of the techniques was to simply recognise and label the type of thought we were having and return our attention to our breath, rather than getting caught up in its story. Common types of thoughts might be:

❖ Fantasising - going off into a daydream

❖ Planning - what you will eat tonight, how you will redecorate your house

❖ Speculating - the "what ifs?"

❖ Judging - includes defining things as good/bad, better/ worse, to destructive criticising, also comparing - she's got more than me etc

❖ Obsessing - thoughts that go round and round, often having an intense angry, violent quality.

In the evening the teacher usually gave a talk expanding on the day's themes. I found the teacher to be remarkably clear, humorous and human and I will always be grateful to her. What she said that night and in the time while I was there had a profound effect on me and has stayed with me to this day. She was expanding on the theme of common types of thoughts. When she spoke about judging and obsessing, I found myself sitting up and somewhat shocked to hear her say, "This is quite simply a form of self abuse!".

As a therapist I have worked with people who have suffered and survived all kinds of abuse. I have passionate reactions of anger, compassion, and disbelief at the cruelty of which humans are capable. I had never equated the kind of daily behaviour I tolerated and perpetrated inside my head with abuse. Had anyone described me as being an abuser, I would have been shocked and outraged. Yet, so many of us find ways to excuse what we do to ourselves as if it were more acceptable than doing it to someone else. There is no excuse for abuse, no matter who it is directed towards, it is still abuse. The teacher's message was simple and direct,"Stop doing it!"

During the course of the weekend I was surprised to observe just how often I had self-critical thoughts. At its most extreme, the onslaught of persecution was continual and the more I tried to return to my breath, the more intense and obsessive the onslaught. I had seen myself as the victim of my thoughts, but had not really grasped that I was also the perpetrator, the Persecutor, as I called it. As I continued to reflect in the weeks and months that followed I began to see how habituated and even addicted I was to my own cruelty; a cruelty I would have abhorred in someone else. I was forced to admit that I even drew a sado-masochistic pleasure in it. I had been all too familiar with my pain and helplessness, but I had never faced my own cruelty.

Listening to the cruel voice, pleading with it, even trying to understand it is pointless and only feeds it energy and encourages its hold on our psyche. The only course of action is to Say "No!" to make a decision to stop abusing ourselves, to recognise and name it for what it is and return to the breath. I practised this over and over, sometimes several times a minute, when self-hate was acute. Each time I refused to listen, to the story, to the sales pitch, another voice inside grew stronger. Eventually that other voice became so strong it gained control and that voice says "Don't do this to yourself!". We have to learn to stand up for ourselves, with ourselves, to get tough and tell that bully in no uncertain terms, to be quiet.

You could if you wish try the 2 by 1 method ! Many years ago I had a client who would frequently tutt and shake her head in self-disapproval, it was as if she were butting her head against an invisible wall. It seemed so casual and harmless, but watching her week after week, I was alarmed at how much she mentally beat herself up. Having drawn her attention to it we devised some homework. I requested that she keep a small length of 2" by 1" wood in her bag and every time she caught herself tutting she had to smack the wood with her hand, so she really felt what she was doing to herself. She soon stopped.

*We Admitted We Were Powerless Over Our Behaviour
And Our Lives Had Become Unmanageable*

Rather like giving up drugs or alcohol, it takes time and patience to stop abusing ourselves. We just have to keep saying "No!" one day at a time. At first we may not recognise our actions until after

Back off!. You don't speak to me like that!

the event. It can take days or even weeks to realise we have been undermining ourselves, that we have expected too much of ourselves. We will, of course, expect ourselves to get it right, do it perfectly, see instant improvement, or beat ourselves up for failing, but that is all part of the self-abuse system. There were many times when I failed to stop the Inner Persecutor and those times would be golden opportunities to beat myself up again for failing. In addition I might then criticise myself for beating myself up! I call this the secondary layer of self-abuse.

I was able to draw from the Twelve Steps of Recovery from addiction in order to counter this secondary layer. Step One is about admitting we are powerless over our own dysfunctional behaviour. And I made this adaptation to use at times when I was overwhelmed by own negativity. Accepting my powerlessness actually allowed me to forgive myself, it forced me to be compassionate towards myself. It began to give me a sense of what it was like to accept my own humanity. In this way the exercise becomes fail-proof! If we succeed in stopping self-critical thoughts then we have the satisfaction of having done so; if we do not manage to do so but we accept our powerlessness, we have a perfect opportunity to practise loving-kindness and acceptance towards ourselves. Either way we are breaking the hold the negative script has over our psyche.

I cannot be sure how long it took but, after a few months,

the gaps became longer and the periods of self-hate became shorter. I realised that it was important not to become fixed on the end result rather to value each time I was able to be kind to myself. Eventually, after two or three years I became aware that I was no longer troubled by the voice of self-abuse. In its place was another voice that was strong and clear in protecting my wellbeing. I recover so much more quickly from those knocks that inevitably arise in life. Even using the sentence I just used, reflects a new ability to take life in my stride, not to see every little setback as part of a personally directed conspiracy to keep me down. Whenever I do something I regret, or when others get at me, I might feel low, but as soon as I start to go down the negative spiral, or persecute myself almost immediately my new voice steps in with, "Don't do that to yourself Rachael!" and I stop.

From the Serenity Prayer used by Twelve Step Fellowships:

> Grant me the serenity
> To accept the things I cannot change
> Courage to change the things I can
> And the wisdom to know the difference
>
> Grant me patience
> With the changes that take time
> Appreciation of all that I have
> Tolerance for those with different struggles
> And the strength to get-up and try again
> One day at a time

Is This A Useful Thought, Does It Support Your Wellbeing?

Another idea that came out of the retreat and changed my life arose from the question above. It was a question the teacher repeated at odd moments during the course of the retreat. It seemed such a basic and practical question to apply to the complex and sophisticated thinking that went on inside my head. Her words stayed with me, and it began to dawn that just because I had a thought did not mean to say it was true. I had come to accept my negative scripts as if they were The Truth, laid down in tablets of stone.

I have always had a strong regard for truth and believed it must always be accepted. But this simple question, 'Is it a useful thought?' was a revelation to me. Even if my thoughts are true, or more to the point, if I believe them to be true I still do not have to accept them. In other words I have the right to question my own ideas if they are undermining to myself. I can choose to believe a truth that nurtures and enhances my wellbeing and I can reject a truth that is destructive to me.

'Is this a useful thought, does it support my wellbeing?' This seemed an excellent question to be asking myself. I wrote little notes to remind myself and posted it on my bathroom mirror, in my purse, on my windscreen, on my computer. Over the years it has become the watchword of my wellbeing, the guardian at my door; if it is useful let it pass, if not shut the door. You might like to use this question yourself and see what happens.

Our negative belief systems are often very skilful at re-asserting themselves. They seduce us into listening to them, discussing with them, arguing with them all the reasons why we should or should not believe what they say. They arouse our curiosity, if only we could understand them a bit better, understand why they are there, where they come from. Maybe there is a hidden key, a last bit of the jigsaw and if we finally understand it we will change. In fact the more we engage with them, the more they sap our energy and weaken our resolve. By engaging with our negative voices we give them credence. By entering into dialogue with them we exhaust ourselves.

Negative scripts are like Bettalife salesmen, they keep pushing their catalogues through the door, trying to sell you all sorts of useless gadgets that they insist will improve your life. If you let them in, they try to persuade you they have your best interests at heart, but it is just a sales pitch for low esteem. The only thing to do is to not engage, say "Not today, thank you!" shut the door and put the script in the bin.

If the voice persists, or tries to argue, just keep repeating the phrase, It's not up for discussion! This is an assertion technique called the broken record, where you repeat your assertion over and over until you silence the opposition. It's not up for discussion, is a phrase I heard used by a colleague when dealing with a client who had very challenging behaviour. I found it to be not only effective in stopping debate, but also deeply satisfying in reminding myself that I do not have to explain or justify myself.

You Have The Unconditional Right To Feel Good About Yourself.
The Moment You realise This You Break The Spell.

I began to recognise that I could go on working on myself forever. I realised that I could go on hoping that if I behaved well enough, if someone loved me/ approved of me enough, if a magic wand appeared and waved over my head - then I would finally be graced with self-esteem. I was in fact seeking a feeling about myself. I believed that self-esteem should naturally and spontaneously emerge from within. Perhaps it is our natural state, if I look at an infant it is naturally open, loving, joyful and unquestioning of its right to be here. But self-esteem is also learned, it is mirrored back to us through the smiles, the responses, the affirmations, the messages given to us by our carers. It is learned from the behaviours displayed by those around us. For those of us who had that affirmation, self-esteem is second nature, we don't have to work at it or consciously think about it.

If, for whatever reason, we were denied that affirmation, we now have to learn how to give esteem to ourselves and practise it consciously. There is no point in waiting for someone to come along and magically grant us what we had the right to be given in the first place. It is too late. Yes, when we were children, we should have been given it by those who were responsible for taking care of us, for parenting and helping us to grow up. But they didn't and no amount of longing, hoping or resenting will change that. We have to do it ourselves.

I thought self esteem was about a feeling but in the end

I came to a conclusion that self-esteem is about a birth-right, the same as food, shelter, or love.

❖ We have a fundamental right to feel good about ourselves! - regardless of how fat, thin, rich, poor, or clever we are.

❖ We have a right to feel good about ourselves - despite our weaknesses, failures, successes, and sometimes dreadful behaviour, Yes including that one you just thought about!

❖ Even if we feel or think badly of ourselves, even in those moments when we are gripped by self-criticism and self-hate, it has nothing to do with our basic right to feel good about ourselves. Self-esteem is a right, not just a feeling.

I concluded that self-esteem is not a result of doing it right, or enough, or some magical final moment. It starts with a decision to esteem yourself, a decision that can be made at eight o' clock on a Monday morning when you are not feeling any particular way. It starts from the recognition that You have the right to feel good about yourself, regardless of your opinions, feelings, or actions. It's not up for discussion ok!

Activities

Say "No!"

❖ Begin to notice the daily words and phrases you use to undermine and abuse yourself.
❖ See if you can identify the inner voice that continually puts you down or convinces you that you are worthless.
❖ Keep saying "No!" and tell it to "Back Off!" in no uncertain terms. Stand up to do this, feeling your strength and determination in your body. Imagine your outrage if you saw someone being

spoken to in the same way and direct your outrage to that inner bully. Start to take your power back. Remember! if you do not succeed, forgive yourself and know it takes time to change.

Meditating on the Breath

This Buddhist form of meditation, called mindfulness of breath, has been used throughout the centuries in many countries. It is designed to loosen the hold our thoughts have over us, to begin to take some charge over our crazy chattering minds. It is a very simple but profound technique and is taught by expert teachers. If you are interested in taking it further, or receiving some instruction in the practice, look in your local area for meditation groups. I have adapted the technique for our particular purposes.

❖ Make a quiet place where you can sit and meditate. You can sit cross-legged or on a chair, making sure you feel supported with a straight back so the breath can flow easily.
❖ If it helps to have a candle or picture that you find conducive to meditation, then do so. Some people dedicate a special place in their home for meditation, making an altar with objects that are sacred to them. These can help to act as a focus towards a more reflective state of mind.
❖ Closing your eyes, or lowering your gaze, start to focus inward. Become aware of your breathing, don't try to influence it, just notice if it is deep or shallow, fast or slow, just let it find its own rhythm. Let yourself become relaxed.
❖ Focus now on each individual breath, just observing the sensation of each breath, as it enters and leaves the nostrils, as the diaphragm rises and falls. Savour the sensation of each breath, this is all you have to do.
❖ Every time you find your mind wandering, just return to the breath. Try not to berate yourself for having wandered, just say, "Great! I woke up again" and return to the breath.
❖ Practice this for 5-10 minutes at first, then lengthening to 15-20 minutes.

Labelling Thoughts

This technique can be added to the breathing meditation or done on its own.

❖ Every time you find your mind wandering, simply label the type of thought, rather than getting involved with what it is saying. Once you have labelled it, simply let go and return your attention to your breath.

❖ You can use this technique at any time, while you are walking, waiting for a bus or cooking. Any time you catch yourself getting caught in negative or destructive thinking, just label the thoughts and let them go.

❖ It does not matter whether you succeed or not each time, just practising it is flexing a mental muscle that you may never have used before.

❖ You can use the labels provided or make up your own, the point is to learn how to stop getting caught in the negative thought patterns that keep you in worthlessness. a) Planning b) Fantasising c) Speculating d) Judging e) Obsessing.

Reward Yourself!

Remember to reward yourself, it should be becoming easier to allow yourself to feel good after reading this, after all it is your right! Stand up to that inner bully who denies you pleasure. Get up and go out. Physical exercise or any physical activity is an extremely important way of shifting your mood, getting you out of your mind and into your body. Simply by moving, you shift negative energy and empower yourself as well as improving your health! Give yourself some strawberries; throw away that old scraggy underwear and treat yourself to some new lingerie, as one person reported doing!

6

Filling The Void With Love

"The person I was before, is now the person I'm looking after. I know I can now depend on myself in times of need."

As we learn to break the spell of self-hate, we can begin to reach the part of us which needs loving and affirming and we can start to let in the love and esteem we long for. We must find the courage to embrace our own inner emptiness, to learn to fill it with love, dignity, respect and all the qualities that would give us a solid sense of worth. We have to be willing to kiss the frog to turn it into a prince or princess. Then we can allow ourselves to nurture and pleasure ourselves, to befriend and protect ourselves.

At the heart of our lack of self-esteem, beneath the layers of insecurity, self-hate and shame there often lies an inner emptiness, a void. It is a sense of emptiness associated with feelings of abandonment and despair. As I wrote in earlier chapters, we often hang onto low self-esteem as a form of defence against the even worse feelings of powerlessness and abandonment. If we have a negative self-image, at least we have an outlet for our rage and frustration and we can direct our passion towards hating ourselves. It gives us the illusion of control over life- events or parents who did not respond to us in ways we needed. It must be because we are bad, or it must be our fault that we are treated so badly.

Underneath all this lies a hidden void, a lack of certainty about our own existence, or identity. This void is waiting to be filled with a solid sense of self, with a sense of being loveable and with a confidence that we have power to affect those around us. As infants and children, we were dependent on others to reflect that sense of self, to affirm us with love and attention. Now we are adults we have to take on the task of building that sense of self from scratch.

For those of us with chronic low esteem, it is hard to start this process. We are probably used to filling that void with negativity, with food, with drugs and alcohol, with work, relationships, with things, with anything we can lay our hands on to avoid the void. We may believe we lack the knowledge, the concepts. We are used to identifying ourselves as small, childlike and as victim. We imagine the task to require some complicated ability that is beyond us.

At the end of the day it is about simply being with the part of us who feels abandoned and unwanted and practising compassion. We have to find the compassion to open our heart to the tiny, terrified and starving infant, to the part of us who feels stupid and inept, to the forgotten child who is locked inside us. Yes that one! Not the perfect one we imagine we should have been. She or he is simply waiting for someone to pick it up and hold it and say, "I am here". That someone has to be us. We have to find the adult part of us who can take charge. When we identify ourselves as the child / victim, we abandon ourselves by ignoring or defending against that part of us which desperately needs loving. We need to learn to turn around and say to ourselves "I am here and I will never leave you". It is the truth after all, we are the one person who will always be around as long as we are alive. One friend of mine expressed this by making a marriage vow to herself, so she would never forget again.

It is sad just how resistant we can be to doing this simple thing, we are so convinced of our own ugliness, unworthiness. The good news is that it only takes one kiss to break the spell. The moment we are willing to take that unwanted abandoned part of us into our hearts, we change our lives forever.

I remember vividly the moment when it happened to me. During a period of time alone one Christmas I found myself descending through the usual spiral of loneliness, depression and negativity and found myself in the void. I was practising a form of meditation which actively works on opening the heart to compassion. I will explain more about this practice and how it can be used to deal with powerful negative feelings. At a certain point during the meditation, I found myself visualising the part of me which was experiencing such excruciating pain and despair. I was somewhat horrified to see the image of a starving infant identical to those from famine-stricken countries and refugee camps. It was wrinkled, with eyes that stared vacantly and every pore of its skin radiated a desperate need. I

felt repulsion and yet I knew I had to pick it up and hold it. The depth of my repulsion was so great I could only manage it for a brief second, using my physical arms as well as my imagination to make the gesture. In that moment I felt compassion for the infant and its suffering and sadness for the repulsion I felt towards myself. There was no instant transformation, but by returning to the image several times that week, I found myself more able to imagine caring for it and feeding it. The shift was subtle and I know that it was a major turning point in my own journey.

When we have low self-esteem we have an all or nothing mentality; either we are competent or inept, we are either perfect or totally unacceptable. It is outside our comprehension that all human beings can sometimes be really stupid and inept and sometimes clever and able and that one does not discount the other. Neither polarity is the whole picture. It is often the childlike and stupid in us that also retains an innocence and openess to life. If we look at society, the most powerful people sometimes make disastrous decisions. Humanity is still struggling to lift its ignorance and errors out of the mire and yet we are also capable of amazing feats. So how can we expect ourselves as individuals to be any different? We certainly do not like or wish to act without intelligence or wisdom. It is distressing to find we have acted with stupidity and it is important that we strive to learn from our mistakes. However, it does seem to be an inescapable part of the human package. So we have no other choice, but to feel compassion for our own humanity, especially if the other choice is eternal self-punishment and rejection. This is it! This is what it is to be human. There is no other place to go, no perfect state where we act impeccably in every situation. As sufferers of low self-esteem we have to give up the illusion that we will conquer all our faults, obliterate all our neediness and vulnerabilities. We are in fact perfectly placed to join the human race and esteem ourselves. Through compassion we feel closer to each other, we transform our brokenness into a state of grace.

Practising Compassion

Many people with low self-esteem find it relatively easy to feel compassion towards others, but extremely hard to experience compassion towards themselves. It is perceived as selfishness, which must be denied. Compassion requires an acceptance of our suffering, a stepping back from that state to a place of a genuine feeling for all of our struggle. Compassion is qualitatively different from self-pity. With self-pity we come from a position of victim and blame, and our heart is closed. It is a self-centred perspective. With compassion we are able to be in the same pain, but our heart is opened to ourselves and to life. We accept our human frailty and in doing so we create self-esteem. Practising and expanding our ability to feel compassion is essential to creating self-esteem. We have to learn to replace our hate with compassion.

I have developed the following Meditation, which I call, "The Heart of Compassion" and I have adapted it from a traditional Buddhist Meditation practice called Metta (translated as Loving-kindness). I have found it to be particularly effective when faced with intensely negative and painful emotions such as: self-hate, anxiety, fear, despair, or neediness. When we are in the midst of such experiences we inevitably perceive ourselves as alone, but if we stop to think about it, we must be one of hundreds of thousands of individuals all over the world who are experiencing that same feeling at any given moment. Recognising this fact lessens our sense of isolation and acknowledges our humanity. The meditation is about using our pain to ask for help for all living beings who are suffering with us.

When we are overtaken by intense states we feel powerless to do anything to help ourselves and invariably we persecute ourselves for feeling so bad. We tell ourselves we are being selfish, useless, indulgent and pathetic. The practice allows us to experience compassion for our own powerlessness and enables us to use our pain in a positive way, by offering it up to life and asking for help for all who are suffering in that moment. In this way we are able to by-pass the Inner Persecutor and open our heart to ourselves.

The phrases are adapted according to whatever you are feeling at the time. Firstly, we ask that we all may be freed from those particular feelings, for example: "May we all be freed from fear. May all beings everywhere be freed from hate." Then we ask that they be replaced by more positive alternatives, for example, "May all beings find peace. May all beings everywhere live with love." The phrases are repeated over and over with each breath, and they become a prayer or chant, sometimes they stay the same, sometimes they evolve as the negativity shifts and dissolves. "May we all be freed from delusion. May we be freed from anxiety. May we be filled with clarity. May we be filled with serenity. May we be freed from worthlessness. May we be freed from despair. May we find our true nature. May all beings everywhere live with love."

As with all meditation practice you will experience it differently each time, according to your mood, or mental state. Sometimes you are filled with peace and stillness, other times you can barely contain yourself to stay with the practice. It does not really matter what you feel, it is doing the practice and not just the experience that counts. In other words meditation is about flexing a mental muscle rather than having a great experience, and if we were restless and distracted, we have not failed. In time that muscle will become a part of our everyday life. Through this practice I have experienced relief from the intensity of the negative feelings and a shift to the ones I wish to replace them with. I have also experienced peace of mind in the knowledge that I am offering something to life.

Activities

Heart of Compassion Meditation

❖ Find a quiet place to sit.

❖ Close your eyes and take some deep breaths, allowing each out-breath to become longer than your in-breath, then let the breath settle into its own rhythm.

❖ Start to bring your attention down from your head and into your heart, feeling the rise and fall of the breath there.

❖ Begin to reflect on the fact that, right now, all over the world, there must be hundreds of thousands of people who are struggling with exactly the same feelings as you.

❖ Allow yourself to identify with them. You are not alone. Recognise that if they are feeling anything like you right now, how dreadful they must feel!

❖ Let the fact so many of us are struggling with the same experience start to evoke your compassion.

❖ Remember! Even though you feel powerless to change what you feel, at least you can do something useful with it. Offer up your pain as a prayer, let it be transformed into compassion.

❖ Use these phrases to name what you feel and what you want to feel instead

❖ May we all be freed from…..

❖ May all beings everywhere be freed from….

❖ May we all find….

❖ May all beings everywhere live with….

❖ Repeat them a phrase at a time with each out-breath. Let your feelings flow, going deeper and deeper into the meditative state and deeper into your heart.

Embracing The Child Visualisation

I described earlier my encounter with my own inner child, the part of me which embodied my lack of self-worth. Visualisation is a powerful tool in providing an arena in which we can dialogue with our inner world, it is also a valuable means of effecting healing and change. For some people visualisation means seeing vivid images, for others it is simply a sense of those images, it does not matter, we are employing our imagination to create healing and to provide an arena where we can dialogue with our inner world.

At a time when you feel ready to embrace your inner child, or the part of you that needs your love, then try this visualisation. I use the term inner child because it is invariably in childhood where the wounds of worthlessness are buried. If you prefer, you can just use the term, "the part of me that feels low self-esteem". This exercise can be very powerful and bring up a lot of feelings, so it is important that you do it at a time when you feel ready.

❖ Sit somewhere comfortable with a cushion close to hand and close your eyes. Take a few deep breaths and sigh, letting go of thoughts and tension.

❖ Allow yourself to become receptive and stay in touch with your compassionate adult self.

❖ Imagine that you are in a place in nature where you feel safe, it may be a place you know or a completely imaginary place. It may be a garden, or by the sea or in the hills. Wherever it is, this is your safe place, a place where things can grow and flow.

❖ Let yourself explore this place, feel its atmosphere, touch the ground, look at the plants that may be there.

❖ Somewhere nearby is the part of you who feels unwanted, who needs love; your inner child. Ask him or her to make themselves known to you. See if you can allow yourself to simply look at this child.

❖ Let the child communicate with you what it needs, either through words or gestures.

❖ Be honest with it about your resistance to accepting it. If you are not ready to take things further, then simply be with each other and imagine a warm shaft of sunlight to shine upon you both. Let yourself open to the possibility of returning another day and bring yourself back to the place where you are sitting.

❖ If you are ready to continue, see if you can find it in your heart to embrace your child, to respond to it. If you have the cushion nearby, pick it up and imagine it is your inner child. Spend some time together holding and comforting each other.

❖ Bring yourself back to the chair where you are sitting.

❖ Allow yourself time to recover, be gentle with yourself. You may wish to continue holding the cushion which symbolises your inner child and to re-enforce your decision to embrace it.

If you have experienced resistance to accepting or embracing your inner child, you can invite the presence of someone you trust who has the love you cannot yet allow. This may be someone you know, or it may be a spiritual being you have faith in. Ask them to join you in the image and ask for their help in this matter.

Sometimes when people do this visualisation the child is found in a dark or frightening place. In this situation you can either transform the place by bringing in the sunshine and blowing the cobwebs away, or you can rescue them and take them away from there to the safe place.

It is important to follow-up the experience in all kinds of ways on a daily basis and that you make a pact with your inner child that you will continue to get to know each other. You can revisit the safe place any time you wish to be with your child. You can play and explore the safe place together. You might want to paddle in the sea if it is part of your landscape, or wander in the garden if that is where you are. See what the child wants to do.

Having an object which symbolises your child, which you can pick up and hold is helpful. It may seem strange, but it works and once you are willing, it can be a pleasurable way of giving love and hugs to yourself. People sometimes buy a soft toy or find some object that they keep with them, to remind themselves of the need to take care of that part of them. Wearing a special jumper, or having a special time in the day to bond and communicate are other possibilities.

Be creative, mess about with paints, make up your own exercises, buy yourself presents, give yourself treats, go for a walk in the woods, sing, dance, kick a football, go shopping for luxuries, anything that gives you joy and makes you feel good. Learn to become a loving parent to yourself.

It takes continued practice to change the long held habit of self-rejection. By talking to our inner child, by playing with it in our imagination and simply remembering it is a precious part of us, it will transform. Now we have some strategies to help us through the wobbly moments, the times when we feel insecure. And if we learn to make contact with that small part of us in moments of anxiety, and listen instead of blanking off or rejecting ourselves,  the panic will quickly subside. Use those times to plant new and positive messages such as;"you are ok as you are, you are special, it's ok to make mistakes, don't worry I'm here, you are safe". When our inner child feels overwhelmed the adult in us can reassure, give comfort and bring in a sense of proportion. We learn to be a kind parent to ourselves. Once we have made contact with it in our imagination the appearance of the child starts to change quite quickly. By changing our behaviour on a daily basis we will start to feel less needy and abandoned and we will gradually fill that void with love.

Weeding And Seeding

This exercise is about letting go of the negative messages you have accumulated from the past. The ones you gave yourself, or those given to you by others. They may have been explicit words that someone said, or unspoken messages implied through someone's behaviour or attitude. This exercise is also very powerful when done with others as a shared ritual. For the exercise you will need a pack of those coloured sticky message-labels.

❖ Write down a message on each sticky label, "You're stupid! You never get it right! Why can't you be more like your sister? All good things come to an end." etc.
❖ Attach each label to your body, wherever feels appropriate.
❖ Look at yourself in the mirror, feel what it is like to carry all these messages
❖ When you feel ready, take each one off with the intention of removing it from your consciousness. Destroy the labels in a ritualised way. You can tear them up, burn them, put them in the bin, offer them to the earth for recycling, whatever way feels satisfying to you. Let yourself feel their absence.
❖ Start to write a new positive affirmation that you want instead, "You are fine just as you are. You are loveable and beautiful. You CAN do it! It's ok to make mistakes, Don't worry it'll be alright! It's alright to ask for help." Start with one and you can add others in time.
❖ You can write your affirmation on sticky notes and post them around your home. Repeat the message to yourself often. Imagine it as a seed you wish to grow. You can visit your safe place and imagine planting it with your child, watering and watching it grow into a flower and trees. You can buy a plant to put in your garden or home as a way of reinforcing your intention to make this new message permanent.

Reward Yourself

Feel free to give yourself as many strawberries as you can manage!

Heart of Darkness

Sometime between breakfast
And the lunchtime post
I slipped through a wormhole
finding myself or some semblance
back in that other universe

and in the terrifying empty
deep black dark
that goes on and on and on and on
in all directions forever
i cannot see
i got left behind
they forgot i existed
so i'm not sure if i do
except the pain that scrapes
the inside of my skin
with a howl as big as a mountain

and in the centre was
is
a tiny spark
that defies the dark
and is warm
and is whole
and is love
and i decided i could
fill myself with it
and i did until it became
the Whole Universe
and I became
and out I popped
joyous to the letters
on the mat

7

How to Stop Lying and Changing What You Do or Say in Order to Please People

"When you discover the sky doesn't fall down if you don't make it better for people, it makes it so much easier."

We all do it sometimes; we might not consciously lie, but are we always completely honest? We are occasionally economic with the truth, we conform and make decisions not to speak out. There are times when having weighed up a situation we make a choice not to rock the boat; that on this occasion it just isn't worth it, or we recognise that little will be achieved by having a confrontation. There are also situations in which we sense it would be unsafe to openly confront someone and we make the wise choice to protect ourselves by remaining silent. In both cases the choice is a conscious one and we remain aware of our personal truth. It is a matter of using our discretion along with the need to honour our truth.

I used to think I was a coward for not always confronting others in a conflict. It was a revelation to me when I discovered that it was ok to walk away and in fact wise to do so when there is no chance of being heard, or met by the other person. I expected the impossible of myself and exposed myself unnecessarily and masochistically to dangerous situations. Afterwards I would beat myself up for not coping better. If I look back on my old behaviour, I realise it was a mixture of having unrealistic expectations of myself, and a misguided and desperate attempt to retrieve my power from people who were skilled at not giving ground.

Having said all this, I know that one of my greatest pains

has been the feeling of letting myself down on those occasions when I have not stood up for myself, or spoken out when someone has treated me with disrespect. In those situations I would go into a shame reaction and be struck dumb. It might have been a situation when someone was sarcastic, or simply being rude and ignoring me. It might be when I had the sense people were talking about me behind my back. My low self-esteem believed it was my worthlessness that caused others to behave badly towards me. Even now that reaction kicks in on occasion and it feels quite disabling. I believe that the sense of betrayal and disappointment, which comes from not defending myself, is a genuine and healthy reaction. We know in our hearts we should honour ourselves and we hurt when we do not. However, if we then tear into ourselves mercilessly and act in self-destructive ways, then that is self-abuse and low self-esteem behaviour. If we are unfortunate enough to have such a disabling reaction, we can recall the first of the Twelve Steps, that at this time we are powerless over our own behaviour and we need to find compassion for ourselves and our plight.

Another reason for not telling the truth is not wanting to hurt someone's feelings. The intention to avoid harm through our actions is one of the values that makes for a civilised society, or at least that we strive towards it. Sensitivity and consideration are considered virtues in a person and if you have ever encountered someone with little or no regard for your feelings you probably found it an unpleasant experience. It is an inevitable part of life that sometimes we do or say things that hurt peoples' feelings. Often it has as much to do with their sensitivities and personal history, as our actions. Sometimes we have to do or say something that we know will hurt another, perhaps because we feel it is for the good of one, other or both parties. It may also be because there is simply no alternative. This is a common issue in close relationships and often what makes a relationship strong is the trust and familiarity which allows us to be so honest with each other. When we find ourselves in such a situation, we usually try to temper our truth with kindness and if we have unwittingly hurt another through our thoughtlessness or harshness, it is desirable that we acknowledge our action and try to make amends.

Again it is all a matter of personal choice and discretion. Sometimes we know that if we do not say something the relationship will suffer, and we will either become distant from each other, or the tension will build up to the point of explosion. Equally, if every little thing is continually picked on and pointed out the relationship becomes insufferable.

You may feel that what I have been saying is obvious common sense, but people with low self-esteem often have great difficulty in these areas. Perhaps we have come to value our truth far less than that of others. Perhaps we have deep fears about what will happen to us if we speak out, or perhaps we have an overdeveloped sense of responsibility for the feelings of others and become wracked with guilt at the thought of hurting someone. We may overcompensate and lose perspective on who is responsible for what.

The same issues of discretion and choice apply when it comes to saying and doing things to please others. When we care for someone we naturally want to please them, to make them feel good; it is one of the delightful benefits of relationships. We call it being thoughtful, and putting others needs above our own has always been held as a virtue, especially for women. The problem arises when we think we have no right to please ourselves or value our own feelings. We lose our sense of discretion and choice when we have to please others all the time, when we can only tell them what we think they want to know. This usually goes together with an exaggerated fear of hurting others or provoking their disapproval.

This is called people-pleasing behaviour and is usually a survival strategy, the way we learned to cope as a child. Pleasing people is a common way of compensating for low self-esteem, after all, how could anybody possibly like us as we are? We believe we have to persuade others to like us by being as nice to them as possible. How could our opinion possibly be of any value? Far better to accommodate other peoples' views and get them to make the decisions.

It can however, be intensely irritating and confusing to be on the receiving end of people -pleasing behaviour; it can also feel very manipulative. Have you ever encountered someone who will only tell you what you want to hear? Someone who always agrees with everything you say, who is always nice and helpful, and who lets you make the decisions, but mysteriously doesn't quite come up with the goods? And when they let you down, they are unfailingly polite, apologetic and understanding,

but then they do it again. After a while you realise that despite appearances these people just cannot be relied upon to give you a straight answer. It sounds like the classic sales-pitch or political manifesto, and we have all met someone like that.

People-pleasing often goes together with passive aggression, because deep down we feel angry at having to suppress our needs and desires. On the surface we appear to comply, whist silently and subtly we resist and rebel; by forgetting, by not turning up, by letting people down. We may also be suppressing a backlog of rage from a past, in which we were punished for having a different opinion. We learned to hide our rage and appear compliant whilst underneath we are still simmering. It may be that we are alarmed by the amount of rage we feel and fear what might happen if we let it out. As therapists we are taught to watch out for the client who constantly smiles, as they are often struggling to conceal anger.

I had a workman in my home. When I met him he seemed very friendly, quick to grasp what I wanted and confident that he had the skills to do all the different jobs required. He even made suggestions as to extra improvements he could make and offered to do them for nothing. I couldn't believe my luck, I thought I had found someone with whom I could work well. At first he worked like a Trojan! One night I came back to find he had cleared up all the mess in the area he was working even though I had not asked him to do so. I expected there to be chaos for a while and realised that he must have worked very hard and stayed late. The next day he arrived late and in a bad mood. He was ill and exhausted and seemed angry with me but would not say anything. He was so ill, he had to go home and did not return for two days, which meant his extra efforts had cost him time. I began to realise that he was desperately trying to please me regardless of his own limitations, and then resenting me for not appreciating his sacrifice. He was martyring himself and making me responsible.

He insisted on doing extra jobs that I did not ask or need him to do, and as luck would have it, there were continual complications with the job I had employed him to do and it was taking longer and longer to complete. He had given me a very good price, again to please me, but the delays meant he was earning less and less. At one stage I was pulled into rescuing him because he had no money to drive here. It was a nightmare; I could never make clear agreements with him because he could not tell me the truth about what he could realistically achieve. He became more and more like a black cloud filling my home with his anger. Each day he told me he would definitely finish the next day and more days went by as he struggled and lied to himself and to me. He could only tell me what he thought I wanted to hear and we both ended up increasingly stressed and annoyed because he could not meet the deadline. The more I got pulled into his complex games the more it drove me nuts! I finally got so stressed, frustrated and angry I could no longer be in the house while he was there and had to insist that he finish that day.

And that is how it is with people who lie to please you; you are lulled into feeling that they will take care of you, seduced into feeling everything is ok. Then you end up feeling frustrated, let down, confused, guilty, angry and responsible. You never know where you are because they cannot tell you the truth. It is like being trapped in a sticky mess.

As children we may have feared that if we told the truth, it would be used against us, or that it would provoke an attack. If another disagrees with us and is strong at holding their point of view, those of us with low self-esteem often cannot hang onto our reality, we start to doubt ourselves, get confused and out of touch with our feelings and thoughts. This can lead to feelings of anger and powerlessness. We might experience a shame attack and go numb whilst trying to make it ok with ourselves. Underneath we feel that deep disappointment and shame for not standing up for ourselves as I described earlier. We may then react with self -destructive behaviour.

Alternatively, if we express an opinion to someone who looks hurt we feel guilty and responsible. We then start to make our own opinion worthless in order to take care of that person's hurt. In other words we take responsibility for their feelings. I remember only too well how I tortured myself for days with guilt and remorse, if someone said they felt hurt by me. It mattered little whether or not it was my action that had caused their upset, I would be desperate to make amends, partly to alleviate the feelings of self-hate and guilt and partly because I had no faith that they would still like me. Even though at an intellectual level I knew it was their stuff, their fear, or their projection, emotionally I felt responsible.

Another word for this kind of behaviour is placating, which is a cross between pleasing and pacifying; especially when dealing with someone who attacks or blames us when confronted. Placating is an attempt to stop someone being critical or angry with us. We will agree with their point of view and do anything they say or want, anything to stop their disapproval or anger. Sometimes this works, but each time we do it, we give away more and more of our power and the other person gains more and more control. Placators usually blame themselves for conflicts, regardless of where the responsibility lies. The partner to this dynamic is the Blamer, someone who automatically points the finger at others in conflict, it is always someone else's fault, never their own. Blamers and Placators make perfect partners, especially in an abusive relationship. As the two positions polarise more and more, the Blamer gains more control, and becomes increasingly aggressive, while the Placator finds their confidence more and more eroded as they continue to give in to the Blamer's demands.

On the surface the Blamer is the one we tend to find the most controlling and unacceptable. However, placating is also a way of manipulating or controlling another's behaviour and can be experienced as highly provocative in the way I described with my story. Both behaviours make it difficult to resolve conflicts, as neither party is able to be honest or take appropriate responsibility. It is, however, important to recognise that both are loyal soldiers, designed to protect and defend our survival and both reactions come from a fear of being blamed.

We invariably have both aspects inside us and Chapter 5, Breaking The Spell is precisely about breaking the cycle of bullying and blame which goes on inside our head. By stopping the habit of placating the internal bully we start to regain our confidence. So by the time you get to this chapter you will hopefully have started to break the habit of people -pleasing!

A common underlying issue to people-pleasing is that of dependency. In other words we have a fear of being separate or different from other people. Our deep irrational fear is that if we were to be emotionally separate we might not survive. It is a fear that comes from very early in our life, when we were physically as well as emotionally dependent. Sometimes, when we have a parent who is themselves emotionally needy and dependent, we might come to believe that if we were to separate from them, it is they who would die.

Either way, being separate spells death to our infant psyche. This manifests itself in small everyday issues; such as having different opinions, reactions, or feelings from those with whom we are in relationship. Being separate brings up the imagined fear that they or we will die and it becomes very hard to have an argument or even do different activities, especially if it is an activity the other person does not like. This is what we call being merged and in this kind of relating we become dependent on other people's approval. I remember how much I was caught in this fear and how I stopped seeing my friends, or doing things I enjoyed, simply because my partner disapproved or was not interested in them. The fear produced when I tried to separate was incredibly powerful; I experienced it like an elastic umbilical cord that sent me zinging back into dependency even at times when I desperately longed to be free.

I recall trying to break up a particularly destructive relationship and over a period of months we must have broken up and made up three or four times. It was a living hell; each time I started off knowing it was the right thing to do and felt good about it. Then within hours I was in turmoil, and obsessed by an unnameable fear that pulled me back into the relationship. Each time I returned I felt more and more humiliated and powerless.

In another relationship this life or death fantasy became very vividly acted out. My partner was physically abusive and as I struggled to part with him, he was diagnosed with cancer. I tried to stand by and support him even though my instincts were to run. As he went into hospital I battled with my fears of what would happen if I left, and also what would others think of me. Inside I secretly wished he would die because it seemed the only way out of this dreadful situation. With the support of certain people I was able to acknowledge my feelings and recognise that I was not in a place to support his recovery. I was able to glimpse that I had a right to protect myself and that I was not responsible for his living or dying, especially as he was being cared for. We both had our own issues to deal with in this situation, nonetheless it was a terrible decision to have to make and I left. We did later get back together for a while, and perhaps it is important to say that he recovered and that each of us in our own way had to make a choice for life and to value that life.

What was a survival issue for us as infants, is no longer a reality now we are adults. Now we are adults we can recognise that we do have the resources to cope. We have to wean ourselves and reassure that part of us that it can survive. Now we are learning to fill our inner void with love we can esteem ourselves. We can remind ourselves that we are no longer at the mercy of a hostile world and that we can survive being different; neither are we responsible for other people's insecurity. If we remember that we have the right to respect and love ourselves, we will no longer fall prey to emotional blackmail, nor will we try and use it against others.

I have spoken to people in their forties and fifties who still react to the World as children. Usually because there is some benefit in staying childlike, such as expecting others to take responsibility for looking after them. However there is also a cost, such as feeling too small and powerless to assert themselves when others push their boundaries. Most people do not even realise that they are behaving in this way and I ask them to remind themselves that they are adults, people with their own experience and authority. By reminding themselves that they are adults and choosing to be grown up, they then feel empowered to stop putting up with others attempts to use and take advantage of them.

While it is important to take other people's feelings into consideration, it is impossible to please others all the time. We have a right to our own view and our own feelings and if others do not like it, perhaps it is their problem not ours. We have the right to say when something does not please us. Perhaps the most important thing is that we have a choice and that we remain honest with ourselves about what we say and do. If we constantly agree and placate others we lose touch with our own truth.

Perhaps we were brought up to think that pleasing oneself is selfish and that selfish means bad! In other words we should only please others and never ourselves. Being able to please ourselves, and being able to be selfish at times when we need to take care of ourselves are all signs of healthy self-esteem. Sometimes we need to say "No" to other peoples' demands, to their friendly persuasion, even to their exciting invitations. Sometimes we need to shut the door, say, "Stuff the World!" and take care of ourselves. Changing our reality to suit others might work as an emergency measure, but not as a way of life. Sometimes we have to accept that whatever we do or say, we have a different reality from our partner and that is ok; the sky will not fall down and we will survive.

Activities

❖ Think of an example where you changed your behaviour in order to please someone. What did you do/not do? What was the price you paid for this? Think of some other examples.

❖ How would you like to be?

❖ What are your fears about speaking the truth? Can you survive differences or do you always have to agree? Can you experience being separate from others or must you always feel merged? What were the messages from your past about these issues?

❖ Use the Activities from chapter six to build your faith in yourself and to learn the skills of reassuring yourself. Our inner child often just needs to be told, "It'll be alright, you can do it!"

❖ Remember that you are an adult now, no longer at the mercy of others, you can make your own choices and you have your own authority.

❖ Take some steps towards being more honest, and build your confidence to say what you really feel:

❖ Start by being honest with yourself; admit to yourself what you really feel, but you do not have to admit it to anyone else. Indulge yourself with a fantasy of really speaking out, of being the teenage rebel and stamping your foot. What is the most outrageous thing you could do or say? Write a letter from "Outraged of Sudthorpe!"

❖ Take a risk by saying how you really feel to someone with whom you feel safe.

Strawberry Time!

Can you do something today that is purely for your own pleasure, just for you? Something that you believe might be really selfish! And something in which you definitely do not have to take anyone else's feelings or opinions into consideration! Count this as your strawberry; in fact have a strawberry feast!

❖

8

What Are These Things Called Boundaries?

"I realised that if I continue to be a victim, if I allow others to mistreat me, I'll always be a victim and I've realised I'm worth more than that! Unless I feel good about myself, others will take advantage of me."

As you learn to break the spell of low self-esteem, you will start to experience yourself as someone who is entitled to love, compassion and respect. This new "you" may feel the need to set new limits for what is acceptable or unacceptable to you. Learning to let go of the need to please others at the cost of yourself will enable you to assert your new boundaries and become less tolerant of others attempts to push you around. Remember the question, "Is this a useful thought, does it support my wellbeing?" We could say that this question itself is a boundary, through which supportive thoughts are allowed, while those that are undermining are kept out. As we recover our self-esteem we may also need to look at how our behaviour affects other people as well as how theirs affects us.

"Boundaries" is a term commonly used by counsellors and therapists to address a number of issues. In their broadest sense boundaries define our personal space, this may be our physical or our psychological space. When someone stands too close to us we will usually feel uncomfortable, and that our physical space has been invaded. If someone is behaving in a needy, demanding manner we can feel that our emotional space has been taken over. Another common area involving boundaries is that of confidentiality; how able are we to keep information to ourselves? When we are upset or anxious, can we contain our feelings or do we feel overwhelmed by the need to rush and tell someone in order to feel better? In a counselling setting the confidentiality boundaries are crucial, for how would we feel safe to open up if we knew our counsellor was gossiping about the things we have disclosed?

Therapists and counsellors talk about maintaining professional boundaries to cover a range of professional conduct. This includes confidentiality, consistency with timekeeping, whether or not to touch a client, refraining from mixing friendship or intimacy with a client, conduct regarding financial payment or entering into financial arrangements other than that of payment for sessions. The main reason for this is to protect the vulnerability of the client and the recognition that a power imbalance exists between them and the counsellor. This is true of a number of professional relationships, such as doctor/patient and teacher/student. When, sadly, boundaries are broken and people suffer mistreatment, at least there is a code of ethics and conduct to acknowledge the fact and to respond to it.

Boundaries serve to protect our vulnerability within relationships and what feels safe or unsafe varies from person to person and relationship to relationship. It partly depends upon the degree of trust and knowledge existing between two people; the less we know each other the more distant and formal we tend to set our boundaries. In intimate relationships boundaries are continually being redrawn and negotiated, this is an integral part of courtship. Just as in the animal realm, courtship between humans can become an elaborate game in which the suitor has to pass subtle tests to cross the next boundary to deeper intimacy. The setting of limits by one party tests and establishes the sincerity of the other and is an important part of creating a safe space for intimacy to take place.

Boundaries help us to organise our experience, a common everyday example being that of time. Time is a collective agreement allowing us to organise our lives and co-operate with each other. Measuring the movement of sun or moon is the means we have evolved to describe the passing of time. People's relationship with time varies from individual to individual and also between cultures. The Swiss, for example, have a very different attitude to those living in India. We all know how we are affected by people who are unreliable timekeepers; however, it can also be difficult if someone is too rigid with their time boundaries.

Having a sense of boundaries also helps us to organise our internal world, to distinguish between thought and feeling, between one feeling and another. Without a sense of internal boundaries it can be hard to tell whether we are angry or sad and whether we are having thoughts or feelings of anger. Having a clear sense of boundaries also helps us to distinguish what belongs to us and what belongs to others. They help us to know whose feelings are whose and who is responsible for what aspect of a situation. Having strong boundaries makes us feel safe and contained, we are more able to detect when we are not being treated with respect and to point out when we feel our boundaries are being pushed or ignored. Having clear boundaries enables us to take care of ourselves, to recognise where our limits are and to say "No" rather than be pressurised or seduced into going beyond them. We know when we are too tired, over-stretched, or out of control. Equally, having a good sense of boundaries also allows us to be sensitive to others. We are able to be more aware of and respect other peoples' limits, to not take advantage of their time or generosity or to break their confidentiality.

Developing Our Boundaries

When we are children it is our parents and later our teachers who define the boundaries. We follow their example but at the same time we start to develop our own and there are two stages of growing up which are particularly associated with this development. One is commonly called the terrible two's, when we start to explore our ability to say "No" and assert our will. Everybody is familiar with the toddler who suddenly becomes obstinate and utters the word "shan't!" at every opportunity. As most parents will testify, another period when boundaries become a daily battleground, is that of adolescence, the teen years. This is the time when we start to rebel, to define ourselves as distinct from our parents and their values. It is a time when we feel the need to explore and test our limits for ourselves and not just take the word of adults. We want to find out what happens when we break the rules and how far we can go without too much risk to ourselves. If we are not met during these stages of development, either by not being given sufficient boundaries against which to test ourselves, or by being suppressed and prevented from having our own view, we will find difficulty with this area.

It is a thankless task for parents during this phase because whatever they say or do it will be wrong. Parents throw up their hands in horror as their little darlings turn into growling, verbally abusive monsters and they find themselves forced to lay down the law about what is and what is not acceptable behaviour. Being the firm but fair authority who sets the rules, is consistent at holding them, then takes the protest and still loves you, is the ideal model. Of course we all find this role so easy to achieve! In most cases families fumble and struggle through this phase emerging somewhere hopefully in the later teens to a different and perhaps more equal relationship between parent and young adult.

The process of finding your own power and authority as a child or adolescent can be complex, as the power relationship is so very unequal. Having a healthy awareness and regard for boundaries between parent and child, helps to safeguard this inequality, just as it does in the professional situations I described earlier. The way a parent uses their authority and power teaches us how to do the same, or the opposite in some cases. If a parent abuses their authority, or indeed lacks it and hands too much power to the child, either way, it damages the relationship with the child's ability to recognise and to hold their own boundaries.

One person I know grew up in a home where her privacy was ignored and her mother and brothers felt free to come into her room without knocking at any time. In her teens she learned to dress in a hurry, listening out in case her brother barged in to get his clothes which were kept in her room. Earlier in the book I described how reversing roles with a parent and becoming their caretaker or confidante can damage the child's self esteem. This is a crossing of boundaries where the child is given too much power and his or her own needs become secondary. One example might be when there is marital conflict and one parent uses the child to offload feelings about their partner. At the opposite end of the spectrum is the rigidly authoritarian parent who punishes without flexibility if rules of behaviour are broken, and who must never be questioned. This can result in the child growing up either as a replica of the parent or as someone terrified to break rules or to voice their own opinion.

Too Much or Too Little

Like everything else we can have too much of a good thing and being too rigid with boundaries can make us inflexible, obsessive and critical. We all know how we feel when we encounter the sort of person called a "Jobsworth" Like everything else we need to exercise a degree of flexibility and discretion. However, lack of boundaries, or boundaries that are too open also create problems. Openness can be a very positive thing, but indiscriminate openness leaves us vulnerable to those who do not have our best interests at heart and who may take advantage of us. We can have a naive kind of trust that the other person knows what they're doing, which leads to disbelief and blame when we discover that they do not. It can make us indiscreet and inappropriate with our personal and private information and again this can allow others to misuse that knowledge.

When we lack boundaries we tend to be chaotic, impractical and inconsistent. It can also make us feel anxious and unsafe. We tend to act on how we feel in the moment and frequently change our plans at the last minute. Invariably this makes it difficult for us to plan anything and we are unable to walk our talk. It also makes it hard for us to take care of ourselves because we have no awareness of our limits. We over-stretch ourselves and are unable to say "No!" when we have reached our limit. This makes us highly vulnerable to being taken advantage of, or persuaded by others. People sense they can get away with it and relying on them to draw the limit for us will not work; hoping that our best friend will know when to stop asking us for favours is fruitless. We have to be responsible for defining our own limits.

It makes it difficult for others to relate to us if we are unable to be consistent, they never know where they stand. If we lack boundaries we can tend to trample on those of other people as well as allowing them to trample on ours. We will be insensitive to their space, their needs and their limits. We may have a habit of interrupting their conversation, or find trouble selecting and focussing on what we want to say and burble on without knowing when to stop.

People with low self-esteem sometimes have a poor sense of boundaries either because we grew up in an environment where boundaries were not kept, or because our boundaries were violated through abuse. It is difficult to have strong boundaries if you have little sense of who you are, it goes together with the territory. With low self-esteem we tend to look to others for affirmation, for approval and for decision-making, after all, our needs, our opinions, our feelings matter far less than theirs. This takes us back to the last chapter on people-pleasing, an issue which frequently goes together with lack of boundaries. The two issues together make a lethal combination which leaves us wide open to manipulation and attack. We can end up being everybody's doormat, failing to recognise that our generosity is a gift to be valued and not abused.

We could also say the reverse, that growing up with a lack of boundaries can create low self-esteem, because we are not equipped with the skills to define and protect our personal space. We feel unsafe, uncontained, defenceless and unable to ground our ideas into action.

Being unbounded can seem very attractive to some people when it becomes confused with freedom. There are those who have a strong resistance to drawing boundaries because they are allergic to being defined, limited or labelled, they believe that to do so would kill their free spirit. This kind of behaviour is sometimes associated with an alternative or New Age lifestyle. Ironically it is only through being able to draw boundaries that we are able to truly be free and have choices.

When we lack emotional boundaries it is harder to distinguish whose feelings are whose, and this can lead us into taking responsibility for other peoples' upsets, problems, and feelings. All of this creates feelings of anxiety, guilt, panic, and self-punishment. We have an overwhelming need to rush in and make things better, not because we care for the other person, but because we cannot bear to feel the pain it causes us. We feel confused, we get so entangled with other peoples' points of view that we end up unable to distinguish what is real and what isn't, what is ours and what is another's. We may even find it hard to define exactly what it is we are feeling and confuse anger with sympathy or laughter.

Another common experience is the feeling of being swamped by our emotions; our anger, or anxiety becomes overwhelming when we lack the skills to contain it. We then resort to getting others to contain our feelings for us by offloading onto them and getting them to listen to us, sometimes for hours on end. We become needy and demanding as we try to ground and contain our upsets.

So how can we change the way we react if we realise that we have boundary issues? Part of the answer is having the information, which is the aim of this chapter. Those of us with poor boundaries mostly lack the education; we do not have the information to know what a healthy boundary feels like. I grew up with parents who were loving, but very unbounded and merged and although I knew their behaviour was unhealthy and frequently made me feel uncomfortable, I lacked the role model that would have helped me behave differently.

I was aware that I too had chronic boundary issues and at times felt ashamed as I sensed how difficult my friends found my behaviour. There were times when I knew I lost friends because they found my uncontained and needy behaviour too difficult. I grew up believing that my honesty and openness were desirable qualities, which they were, but I lacked discrimination and made myself unnecessarily vulnerable. I would be indiscreet because I needed to be liked and when I felt anxious or upset, I immediately needed others to help contain my feelings. I knew this was demanding and tried to spread myself through several friends who I felt could tolerate my anxiety. I also suffered the disappointment and shame of not being able to stand my ground when others pressured me or opposed me. To compensate for this I developed a tough, over-confident front, so I appeared to be very assertive and friends had difficulty believing I could be bullied. But it was a front and once someone got past my initial defence, especially if they were assertive and most especially if they were someone whose love and approval I needed. I was a pushover.

As a child I suffered through the lack of boundaries around me, I felt taken over, swamped, and at the same time indulged and unsafe. Not being challenged and being set stronger limits, when I was older, left me feeling very free but paradoxically unsafe and I was arrogant and dismissive towards my parent's authority. There was no-one around to ask, "Excuse me but can you teach me about boundaries?" No lessons existed on our school curriculum. Besides, I did not have the words to know what I needed and I was far too ashamed to ask for help. What I did was to observe, and hang out with those people who seemed to be good at it and try to learn from them. Sometimes it was painful as I could feel their energetic "No!" quite strongly if I hit one of their boundaries. Invariably it felt like rejection and I usually had a shame reaction, but at the same time I was relieved and grateful that someone had shown me a boundary and the kind of energy needed to hold it in place.

I envied people who seemed to know when others were going too far, for I lacked that ability to know when someone was mistreating or crossing my boundaries. Often it was only through the reactions of friends, who pointed out to me that I had taken advantage of them, which made me aware of the fact. It was a real handicap.

So, finding role models to show us what healthy boundaries look like is important. However, it was not enough to help me understand my history and heal my pain around this issue, I needed the help of a therapist. Counselling can be very helpful in educating us about boundaries and I know that being a therapist myself has been a constant source of learning about the wisdom of good boundary skills.

Books are another source of information and those dedicated to recovery from addiction can provide help, for boundary issues are quite common amongst those suffering from addiction. This is particularly so of books on co-dependency and you will find some titles at the end of this book.

As one client informed me, it is our instincts which tell us when we are being pushed or invaded. In which case we have a natural sense of our personal territory. I tend to agree with this idea but I am still testing it out. Certainly when I compared my own non-reactions to others very quick and automatic response to being pushed or manipulated, it felt clear that I lacked something, an instinctual alarm bell. And this has felt as much of a handicap as not being able to read without glasses. So, how is it that some of us lack this protective alarm bell?

This client put it so very well, "I learned to desensitise myself, my boundaries were continually ignored and occasionally violated. I learned to numb my instincts, I thought that to not feel would put me in control. Instead it cut me off from the feedback signal that told me this is unacceptable. Now, when my boundaries are violated I'm aware that I don't do anything and afterwards I go over and over what I would have said or done and rehearse for the next time, but I never do it."

How many of us can identify with this experience? I know how familiar it has been for me, and how over the years, I persuaded myself that that voice did not matter. Sometimes out of the need to be accepted, out of fear of conflict, out of habit and gradually that voice that said "this doesn't feel right", became smaller and less significant. If in fact we have simply lost touch with our instinctual awareness of our boundaries, then surely we can recover it and learn to recognise the signals again. For example, feeling confused with someone can indicate that their confused boundaries are affecting your sense of reality. Next time you feel that someone is pushing you around and you tell yourself, "It doesn't matter"- know that it is a sign to do the opposite.

More than anything, having a sense of self-esteem will put you in touch with what makes you feel good and what doesn't. You will start to notice more clearly where your limits are and begin to claim your right to assert your limits both with yourself and with others. You will be less tolerant of hanging around people whose lack of boundaries undermines your own. Each time you set a boundary where it is needed, you will feel better about yourself and gain the confidence to do it again.

Saying "No" to people can be scary and, yes, they may well get upset. We have to learn to stop feeling guilty every time we say "No" to someone, but if we can stop listening to the bullying voice inside we can stop listening to the guilt-making one as well. Remember the question, 'Is this a useful thought, does it support my wellbeing"? The trouble is that if we do not say "No" when we need to, others will inevitably take advantage of us, either because they do not know where our limits are or because they know they can get away with it.

One person I knew had been separated from her partner for a year, she was living in her own house, but he had a key and would turn up to see the children whenever he felt like it and stay to tea. Once she realised how this was undermining her and found her sense of right to say "No" her confidence changed. She was able at last to move on from the broken marriage, she stopped feeling depressed, bought new clothes and decorated her home. She enthusiastically set about experimenting drawing boundaries in other situations. Her children had been used to coming into her bedroom and watching her television while playing, despite the fact that they had one in their own room. I suggested she might like to reclaim her room as her sanctuary, which she did with relief. She discovered that if she stated her boundary with clarity and without concern for the other person's reaction, they seemed to accept it without a fuss.

Activities

❖ How well do you relate to boundaries? Are there some areas in your life where your boundaries are stronger or weaker than others? eg with authority figures, in intimate relationships, gossiping/ indiscretion.

❖ How would you like your boundaries to be? What do you need to change? Start with one small step: clear clutter from your home; structure your time so you have space for yourself as well as others; tell your friend next time she turns up without notice, that you are not able to baby-sit, or cut her hair, or that you will only listen to her troubles for a limited time.

This Is My Space!

❖ Use this affirmation as your declaration to the world. It is best said standing with your feet firmly planted on the ground.

❖ Feel the earth energy surging up through your legs. Put your arms out in front of you with your fingertips touching to create a circle of space.

❖ To re-enforce this boundary, declare it to the four compass directions drawing an imaginary circle of protection around you. The tradition of calling a sacred circle comes from pagan traditions around the world. You stand in the centre and point to each direction in turn, calling upon traditional elements and energetic protectors of each quarter. This varies with different traditions, and you would need to investigate those traditions, but here is one suggestion.

❖ Face to the North and ask for the protection of the earth and its gift of stability and standing your ground.

❖ Then turn to the East calling in the energies of air to hear and protect you as you declare "This is my space!". Think of the qualities of this element, of clarity and space.

❖ Turn to the South, calling in the protection of fire and its qualities of passion and power.

❖ Turn to the West calling in the protection of water, with its ability to flow and cleanse.

❖ Return to the North to complete your circle and feel the earth strongly again.

This exercise can help you feel calm and solid when you are feeling a bit panicky. Use the affirmation "This is my space!" at every opportunity and say it loudly and clearly.

Reward Yourself

Do I still need to mention the word treats? Or are you now hopefully in the habit of "loving yourself up" at every opportunity?

9

Blurred Edges

"I've finally found the strength to stand up for myself and it makes me feel good! People around me are getting the message - it's time to grow up! And hopefully if my daughter sees me doing it, she might learn to stand on her own feet at last."

Words have such a powerful effect upon our psyche; when we reflect on the messages we carry, the "weeds" and the "seeds", we recognise how much those words have influenced our confidence and self-image. Words like "stupid", "useless", "should" and "fault". We also have a tendency to confuse certain words that seem similar, but which have subtle yet profound differences. These differences have an impact on us and on our outlook. This chapter looks at pairs of words that particularly relate to issues of self-esteem and explores the meaning and implications those words carry. The words I have chosen are either close in meaning, or they are frequently found together as different aspects of a particular experience. You may find you disagree with my interpretations, nonetheless you might find it useful to think about how you use some of these words and what they mean to you.

Responsibility v Blame

Responsibility means simply owning something. When we take responsibility for our behaviour or for an action we are saying, "This belongs to me, I did this". Responsibility does not imply any criticism or judgement it is simply a statement of causality. I know that if I feel angry with somebody, or hurt by their behaviour, and they acknowledge responsibility for their part in it, I then find it much easier to forgive that person and to let go of my feelings of hurt. If they deny responsibility for their action, it is as if I have to continue carrying my feelings of hurt and also the energy of their behaviour. It is much harder to move forward and I feel stuck with the situation, which is extremely uncomfortable. Unfortunately it is very common for people to be unwilling to take responsibility for their actions, either because they fear the consequences, or because they confuse responsibility with blame. How many of us experience the frustration when trying to make a complaint and we are faced with, the "it's nothing to do with me" syndrome in businesses and organisations. How simple and timesaving it would be if organisations and governments, owned up when things go wrong, instead of denying, covering up and passing the buck.

One of my favourite definitions of responsibility is "our ability to respond to Life". I like it because it emphasises the empowering aspect of taking responsibility for ourselves and our choices. If we refuse to take responsibility, we become the victims of our experience and we cannot make choices. Equally, we need to be able to discriminate between what we are and what we are not responsible for. Sometimes we find that hard and end up taking too much, as well as too little responsibility. This is a common complaint of those who suffer with low self-esteem. Again I think that the confusion with blame is often at the heart of this. Whilst we may be responsible for an action which has hurt someone, we are not responsible for their feelings. A subtle distinction, but one that allows us to face the truth and to make amends without allowing ourselves to be demolished. I have struggled with this concept myself, for it is easy to say and much harder to do. When someone accuses us of making them unhappy, hurt, or angry; it is difficult not to feel responsible for their feelings of hurt. Perhaps reminding ourselves that we are powerless to control another person's behaviour or reactions can help us to retain this perspective.

Blame on the other hand, is a form of judgement and punishment. We often add blame to responsibility and instead of thinking "I did this", we take it to mean "I'm bad, for doing this." Blame carries the energy of anger and shame about it.

Blame is very much a finger-pointing activity either at others, or ourselves. It is perhaps an attempt to pass the pain around, the hurt and anger resulting from an action. If we point our finger at others then we are saying, "You're responsible for what happened. Here! you can carry all the pain and the badness for it." We are also saying, "It's nothing to do with me!" If we blame ourselves, we are saying, "It was all to do with me, I'm the bad person, I deserve to be punished for it all, I will be angry and ashamed of myself for a while to make up for it."

In conflicts we can get locked into blaming each other for what happened, locked in a never-ending and fruitless battle of tit for tat. This usually results in more pain, more tearing each other apart and almost never in resolving the argument. What invariably happens is that the parties eventually tire of the battle and decide to stop and either never see each other again or start talking to find another way of dealing with the problem. This sadly applies to countries as well as individuals.

Blame is actually a way of avoiding responsibility; it is a victim's game. As long as we are blaming someone for what happened to us, we do not have to face up to what we can do about it, we do not have to deal with our feelings, or the part we may have had to play. As long as we blame someone for what happened to us we are tied to that person; we are never free. We have given them all the power over the situation and we need to keep mentally replaying the conflict and feeding our resentment towards them in order to justify the blame. Forgiving does not mean forgetting, it means letting go of the feelings, the emotional charge we have around a conflict. It allows us to move on. We may not condone someone's behaviour but we need to stop rubbing the salt into our own wound. It also means that we need to examine our own part in a situation. Much as we try we cannot control other people's behaviour, but we can do something about our own and we can still make choices. Remember Dr Jerry Jampolski's words, "Do you want to be right or do you want to be free?"

What would happen if you started to separate your use of these words? What would it mean to you if you allowed yourself to feel responsible without feeling blame? You might want to practice saying "I did this", or "this belongs to me" as a simple fact, in the same way that you would say "this is my pen" or "that is the door". You might find yourself thinking "I did this and I feel bad about it", but does it make a difference if you distinguish these words from one another?

Approval v Recognition

These two words can appear to be very similar, yet we think we are seeking one when in fact we need the other. Approval is a word that means "Well done!" "You did it right" "You did it enough". For me, approval carries with it a judgement, a how much, a standard that is measured by the approver. If we are caught in seeking approval, we project it onto others to whom we give the power to decide whether we meet the mark. We create them into being the one who gives us permission, to do or even to be whatever it is we seek their approval for. It can be expressed by directly asking or by those subtle little glances with the eyes, to check that what we are doing is ok.

The trouble with approval-seeking is that it is all consuming and it exists mostly, if not all in our heads. Our thinking becomes obsessed with imagining what others are thinking about us. It is a very self-centred activity and of course frequently inaccurate. We are entirely convinced that what we imagine is so, yet how can we possibly know what others are thinking? Even if we are right, we cannot control other people's thoughts, they will approve or disapprove according to their own reactions and their own concerns. Based on these fantasy projections we will dress and behave in ways that we think will win the approval of others, or at least stave off their disapproval. In fact others are invariably concerned with their own issues and are unaware of our anxieties. Being with someone who is constantly seeking your approval can feel very uncomfortable, partly because you feel they are making you responsible for things you cannot be responsible for and partly because it is so self-absorbed.

Approval leaves the power and authority in the hands

of others. At the same time, the source of approval/disapproval is actually an internal figure which we project onto others; their opinion simply triggers our own inner approver. Having said this, our fears usually stem from somewhere, or someone from our past who was constantly critical or discouraging towards us. Gradually we internalise their voice until it becomes a part of the software inside our heads.

In contrast, recognition is about being seen and heard as we are, about being recognised for our actions. It is a bit like responsibility, in that it is a statement of "you did this" "you are this", "I hear you", "I see you" "I understand you".

I mention these two because, at a certain time in my life, I was struggling with trying to stop myself from seeking approval. I condemned myself for this activity which took so much time and energy and irritated both me and my friends. I sought approval by performing and entertaining, by being clever and by being helpful. It was all to do with what others had praised me for, for the talented little girl that they loved to boast about. In fact it was not winning me friends at all, rather it made me act in a forced way and I was a show-off. I suddenly realised that what I really needed was recognition, recognition for who I am, not for what I could do. I simply wanted to be seen and heard as "me". Once I understood this I was able to ask for recognition in more appropriate ways and also to learn how to give it to myself. So to me approval is more to do with other people, whereas recognition is more to do with myself.

Longing v Love

I have written at length about longing and love in chapter four and how we substitute one for the other. As I have said, longing has an intensity and craving about it. It becomes a never-ending means of holding satisfaction, or disappointment at bay. The trouble is, we can become attached and even addicted to longing as a state of being, to the feeling of craving. Perhaps because our original longing for love was not fulfilled and then longing became the nearest substitute. In this way we will sabotage all efforts to fulfil our longing, usually unconsciously, by choosing objects of longing that are unavailable. We grow used to romantic fantasy and idealisation as a way of denying our feelings of disappointment, rejection and abandonment. Longing can also be a great motivator, a great, big eternal carrot to keep us hooked. Longing can, for example be a feature of a person's spiritual path, a divine homesickness as it were, a longing for unity, for Nirvana. And in its positive sense, provides a great motivator to keep seekers seeking the truth. As in the legend of the Holy Grail, finding it was not the point, it was the truths discovered on the quest that mattered.

Love is perhaps beyond my ability to define and I am sure many of you will have your own definition. As I understand it, Love is a force of the Universe, it gives us a sense of belonging and wellbeing. Without love or some hope of love we cannot survive as human beings, we starve emotionally and spiritually. That is why we strive in such extraordinary ways to find love, at the cost of ourselves, our lives, our families, our beliefs. Perhaps what I am talking about here is longing, the longing for love that drives us to overcome all odds and also to despair. However, we need to draw a distinction, to avoid blurring the edges between love and our longing for it. Love is; it embraces and holds, love accepts, it fights and it forgives, love gives and it receives. Love allows us to overcome our prejudices and our differences. Love expands and encompasses, whilst longing is single-minded and fixed upon the object of its desire.

Modesty v Denial

I have often heard people talking about the need to be modest as a virtue. This is particularly true in the Christian tradition and those in religious orders take a vow of humility as a part of their initiation. Modesty is by nature a quiet virtue, humble people need no acclaim or recognition for their deeds, they are content to sit back and let others take credit. People who are modest feel a sense of being a part of creation, without needing to assert their place. They do not need to seek power, or as we would say in modern parlance, they are not on ego trips.

Unfortunately it can also be used as a means of self-denial, something people with low self-esteem are particularly good at. Modesty can be used in a very self-punishing way to humiliate ourselves and to never allow ourselves to rejoice in our attributes, our achievements or to take pleasure at all. The same could be said for humility. People with low self-esteem who find it hard to stand up for their rights, and their needs can think they are being modest when in fact they are allowing themselves to be humiliated or abused by other people.

We all need to be able to deny ourselves sometimes, and to put others first, but there has to be a balance. True modesty does not allow itself to be trampled on, it does not belittle itself and will stand up for justice. Modesty simply has a sense of perspective about the bearer's place in things.

Selfish v Self-centred

The word Selfish is such a loaded word in our society, as if being selfish makes us a horrible person. People with low self-esteem often have a horror of being selfish, or at least of being accused of being selfish. They use the word selfish with which to beat themselves, and they use it to deny all or any of their needs. Selfish generally means looking out for number one, but because the word has such negative associations I have found the phrase, taking care of myself, to be a more acceptable substitute. It allows me to honour the fact that I have a right and indeed a responsibility to take care of myself and to take care of my needs. If I do not, then I am expecting someone else to do that when as an adult it is my job. If I do not take care of myself, at worst my health will suffer, at the least, I will become stressed, needy, joyless and resentful.

Some people like to call this healthy selfishness. We all need to be selfish sometimes, to say, "No", to shut the door on the world and replenish ourselves, to not listen to others' demands, or problems and to not go to that extra meeting when we have no more energy left for others. Sometimes we need to treat ourselves and know that it is just for us, no-one else. Sometimes we need to risk others feeling rejected, upset or even annoyed when we say, "I'm sorry but I have to take care of me! I need some space." Other people benefit when we know how to take care of our needs, we are less needy and have more to give. As you feel your self-esteem grow more robust, try saying aloud some day, "I'm going to be really selfish and do... ,or give myself...."

Self-centred, on the other hand means to be focussed only on your own needs and to be completely aware of other people and their needs. Children are self-centred, they are the centre of their own universe and everything exists for them. This is how nature has designed it and to a large extent it works. Childhood is a time when we are devoted to our own development, to growing our bodies, to learning about our environment. It is not our job as children to be worrying about the responsibilities of life. It is the parent's job to take care of our physical and psychological needs until we are independent enough to take care of ourselves. Learning to recognise that we are not the only ones and that we need to share and to consider others is all a part of growing up. However, there are adults who have not learned this, who are still mental toddlers demanding that their needs be met, regardless of others. There are those who may be charming, but exist in a state of self-importance, believing that their interests and their opinions are of prime interest to everyone, while the views and interests of others are of minor insignificance. Self-centredness is more to do with a state of maturity.

Power v Control

Power is another highly loaded word, so often we experience power as control, as having power over another. The two words are closely found together, and yet there are important distinctions between them. Those who have control have the power, and those who have power use it to control others. People with low self-esteem often have difficulty with owning their power, because they have experienced the abuse of power, or have been discouraged from expressing theirs. They will reject or deny their own power at the cost of their health and safety. Women have traditionally been expected to be the enablers and have been discouraged from owning their power. Men on the other hand have in the past been expected to be powerful, to compete and claim their power in the world. In the last few decades these expectations have been undergoing change but the conditioning still lies deep and individuals still struggle to break the taboos they grew up with.

The trouble with denying our power, is that it will seep out in unhealthy ways. Often it makes us more, rather than less controlling; remember the people-pleaser! People who martyr themselves, or who identify strongly as victims can also be very controlling of others. Martyrs have a powerful way of making you feel guilty for doing or being what you want to do or be. Victims can also be very draining and demanding that their needs have to be constantly met. It is ironic that people who are controlling often perceive themselves to be without power. They often attempt to control situations out of fear and anxiety.

Perhaps if we were to think of power, as standing firmly in our own reality, it might free us from linking it with the dreaded "C" word. Another way of distinguishing between the two words is that power can be shared, whereas control cannot.

Giving v Sacrifice

Generosity is a virtue that we all recognise, the willingness to give, to offer, to help. However it can be used as a means of compensating for low self-esteem. We might believe that if we give enough, people will love, approve, or like us better. Giving can become excessive, even oppressive if it is not balanced by receiving. It can become a manipulation when used to buy people's affection. Sometimes we give in an attempt to demonstrate what we would secretly like to receive but dare not ask for. In a similar way that I described in the chapter on people-pleasing, giving becomes a problem if we are unable to give to ourselves. It is when giving crosses over into sacrifice that it becomes a problem. The archetypal image of the self-sacrificing Mother who is tirelessly there for her children, requiring no thanks and no time off, is one with which we are familiar. However, such sacrifice can be hard to live up to, it can make us feel guilty and forget that it is their choice. This is especially true when we are told that they are doing it for us. The person may secretly, or unconsciously express resentment and neediness by comfort-eating, by being ill, or by guilt-tripping. Like the joke, "How many mothers does it take to change a light bulb?" the answer being, "Don't worry about me, I'll just sit here and suffer alone in the dark!"

Detachment v Dissociation

These are not words we commonly use but the distinction between them might be worth examining. Detachment is an important ability, we need to be able to step back from situations and from our feelings. Detachment allows us to gain perspective on different and sometimes conflicting experiences, it allows us to deal with crises in a calm and rational manner. It can also be used as an extreme defence when we are unable to cope with the intensity of our experience, a painful memory, or when we feel powerless and out of control. In these instances detachment becomes a cutting off, or dissociation from our feelings. This is a fear reaction to an experience which threatens our survival and is common to people who have experienced abuse or rape.

As a temporary measure it works and allows us to survive the experience. It may be very necessary to switch off when we are unable to cope with dealing with the shock and pain of a trauma. The trouble is it tends to become a permanent habit leaving us in a vulnerable and dysfunctional state. We switch off and energetically leave our body in an attempt to feel safe. In fact by dissociating we leave ourselves more open to attack and abuse. It makes it harder for us to connect to our feelings and thoughts when we do need them, and unfortunately it cuts us off from the good feelings as well as the bad ones. The description of a shame attack in chapter three could be a description of dissociation. Using drugs and drink to cut ourselves off from painful memories is a common way of dissociating. Can you remember way back to chapter two when I described people who have a deep ambivalence about being born into the physical world? People with these issues of extreme sensitivity to life often tend to cultivate this form of escaping, of switching off from reality.

It is a relief to be able to step back, to observe our feelings and to observe a situation; however it is also important that we do not become so removed from our experience that we are unable to retain our compassion and sense of connectedness. The word that the Buddhists use to describe this quality is equanimity and it is a spiritual quality that they strive to attain. Equanimity is that ability to stand back, to be non-attached or neutral to ones feelings, thoughts, or the outcome of a situation. However it is not a cold place, it is a compassionate, tender place and the best way I have heard it described is "Being equally near to all things". People in the world of addiction recovery would call it serenity as quoted in the Serenity Prayer earlier in this book. Serenity and equanimity are very peaceful states, they are not cut-off, they are in touch with experience and with feelings but not lost in them.

With many of the words I have attempted to explore in this chapter, it is a question of distinction, of not blurring the edges where one word crosses into another, altering its meaning and experience. Some of the pairs are so entwined that it is hard to separate their use and meaning. However, it is useful to try and be clearer and to empower ourselves to create the kind of behaviour and experience that enhances our self-esteem and wellbeing.

Activities

❖ How do you experience these words? What happens when you change the way you use them?

10

Love Yourself Up!
Maintaining Self-Esteem

"I'm no longer a nobody, I have a life and I know there are people out there who care for me."

By now you have begun to break enough of your barriers to self-esteem to be able to let in some praise and compliments. Hopefully, now you can start to let in the good things, the thoughts, actions, words and experiences that nourish and support your positive sense of self. Feel free to congratulate yourself, you have begun to change the habits of a lifetime and are creating a more positive direction for yourself. Remember the second verse of the Serenity Prayer.

> Grant me patience
> With the changes that take time
> Appreciation of all that I have
> Tolerance for those with different struggles
> And the strength to get-up and try again
> One day at a time

It does not matter how long it takes you; there is no race. Each of us is different, we have different histories and patterns to deal with. Some people will find that the methods described in this book work within days, for others it may take months to see a marked improvement. But each time we manage to stop beating ourselves up, each time we are able to treat ourselves with kindness and forgiveness, we are reclaiming our birthright; our right to feel good about ourselves as we are. Remember, one of the characteristics of low self-esteem is expecting too much of ourselves, demanding impossible standards and refusing to allow ourselves any mistakes. The opposite of this is to affirm ourselves for the efforts we have made, to enable ourselves to keep going with words of encouragement, and tell ourselves that we will succeed in time. If we recognise that we will not succeed in a situation, we can honour ourselves and reassure ourselves a) that we are allowed to fail, it does not mean that we are bad. b) it is not we who are wrong, but perhaps it is the course of action that is wrong for us.

A prime example of this is when a relationship breaks up. It is so common to blame ourselves for the relationship not working, to convince ourselves that it was our fault, that we are just not loveable, otherwise we would still be together. "Is it useful to tell ourselves this? Does it support our wellbeing?" Relationships fail for all kinds of reasons and none of them mean that we are unworthy of love. We need our self-esteem more than ever when we are hurt. When others reject us, we sometimes do something that only prolongs our pain, we reject ourselves. We shut ourselves out of our own heart and cut ourselves off from the very source of our own healing. We must learn to keep our hearts open, to ourselves at least so we can salve our wounds and give ourselves TLC. It was the relationship that failed, not us. We need to say "Don't do it to yourself!" when we are tempted to put ourselves down. And then we need to go out and give ourselves a strawberry, something that makes us feel good inside.

This is a poem I wrote to a friend after her relationship broke up, anything just to get her to laugh and hang onto her self worth.

> When life feels blue
> Just say, "POOH!"
> And don't let the b.......s get you

Wear lots of pink
Have forty winks
Or cakes, if that's what helps you

Plant some seeds
Or string some beads
And with every one say "Bless you"

Paint your room
Or take a broom
And clear out all that stops you

Feel free to chant
Or buy a plant
Or anything that suits you

Plot vengeance schemes
Have fabulous dreams
Anything that tells you

You're the best and they're the worst
Just don't let the B........... GET YOU!

Just as it takes daily effort to maintain low self-esteem, so we need to continually maintain and preserve the positive sense of self we are acquiring. Instead of beating ourselves up every hour, we need to affirm and nurture ourselves, to feed ourselves with things that make us feel good. Treating yourself to a break, a walk in beautiful surroundings, letting in a compliment, saying nice things to yourself, letting others support you, are some of the things you might have to do to keep your self-esteem pot topped up. Terrible homework I know, but I am sure in time you will get used to it! And if you keep up your strategies when times are good, you will have plenty to fall back on when they are not. People with low self-esteem sometimes have a habit of abandoning themselves and it is important not to do so. One example might be, stopping our interests when we are in a relationship. Alone times are also important for replenishing ourselves.

This book offers suggestions that I have used with myself or with others. I hope that you have found them helpful but you will also have plenty of your own ideas about what works best for you. It is important to collect lots of different strategies to help you to recover and maintain your confidence. Once we learn how to create self-esteem, we need to make sure we safeguard it. As one client put it, we need to become the guardians of our own well being.

Collect simple affirmations, positive thoughts that inspire and remind you to esteem yourself. Some examples might be: "It's ok, it will be alright! I am Rachael and that has to be good enough! This is MY space! One day at a time." Books and poems that inspire are also enjoyable ways to keep a positive attitude. It is all a matter of personal taste, I have used some poems throughout this book and listed other books at the end, but you will find your own. Music and songs are also a very important way of giving yourself a lift when you need it.

Write a love letter to yourself! On a good day when you are able to appreciate just what a special person you are, write a letter to yourself, using your name often. Tell yourself all the things you appreciate about yourself and say comforting things you might say to someone who is feeling a little low. An example might be, "Dear ....., I just want to say how much I appreciate your generosity of spirit, your courage in facing painful truths. I know you might not feel it right now but you are special and you are loved. I know things might look bleak right now, but I want to remind you of the times when .... (name positive memories)." Seal your letter and on a day when you are feeling low you can open your letter and read it to yourself.

Visual images are another way of enhancing a positive outlook, a postcard, painting or picture that makes us feel good and gives us a sense of beauty. You can also close your eyes and allow an image to come that symbolises self-esteem to you. You can then use that image every time you want to remind yourself of that quality. It can work really well to draw or paint your image and put it up at home. It is possible to extend this to any positive quality we want to develop in ourselves, or our lives. For example if we want to develop courage, we might find a particular animal that symbolises that quality; a lion, or even a rabbit might be the key to the courage we need to find. We can use our imagination to visualise that animal and ask it for advice (using the visualisation in Chapter 6 as a framework).

The image of a wise being is another symbol that we can draw on. This might be a figure from a spiritual tradition that we connect with, such as Buddha, the Goddess or Christ. Spiritual faith can play an important part in our recovery, especially if we can draw upon qualities of compassion and love.

Many women, including myself, have found a positive sense of themselves as women and of being powerful women and priestesses, through re-discovering Goddess-centred spirituality. Men too have found affirmation of their feminine side through meeting the Goddess. The Divine Feminine and her associations, such as the body, sexuality, the earth and the natural world, have for centuries been suppressed and degraded by patriarchal-based religious traditions. Tragically this led to persecution and negative perceptions of women, and has deeply affected our psyche and self-esteem. Thankfully this is changing, although much remains to be changed. Women priests are slowly becoming accepted in at least two of the leading world religions and there is recognition of the need to redress this imbalance. By celebrating the seasons, honouring all life forms and honouring the Divine Mother in Her many aspects, we connect to something deep within our psyche. Our whole attitude towards the Earth is being overturned as climate change forces us to look at our exploitation of and lack of respect for Mother Nature.

Nevertheless, some people find any religious associations difficult and carry associations of guilt and sin, or feelings of worthlessness and imperfection. These people may prefer a more abstract image such as the sky or sea. It could also be an inner figure which symbolises the wise part of ourselves such as an Old Wise Woman, or Man. Equally it could be our Inner Child who carries the wisdom we need at that time.

Wear colours, eat foods, and decorate your surroundings in ways that reinforce the positive qualities you want in your life. If orange makes you feel good, wear it, eat it, have orange flowers in your garden. If pink makes you feel loved, do the same, buy pink underwear, a nice piece of rose quartz crystal. Whatever it takes to "love yourself up".

Physical exercise or any physical activity is a great way to make you feel good. Gardening and putting your hands in the earth, decorating, walking; anything that gets you out of your head, into your body and gets you moving. It can help to shift the most stubborn malaise as it stimulates endorphins. Added to which it improves energy and health. Creativity is another means of transforming negative energy. A lot of the exercises in this book involve creative activity, writing things down, writing poetry, singing, listening to music, dancing; anything that affirms your self-expression.

At the same time we might need to refrain from old ways of comforting ourselves, habits that we now recognise as unhealthy. Retail therapy, or going out and buying things, is a very popular way of making yourself feel better. However, if you have been using this in an addictive way, to avoid facing reality, or in an uncontrollable way that leaves you in debt, then you might need to refrain and appreciate what you have. Binge eating, or drinking might no longer be the best way of rewarding yourself. The act of limiting these old behaviours then becomes an act of self-esteem.

Choosing who and how you relate to others is also important. You may have been in the habit of commiserating with others who suffer from low self-esteem and whilst this can be supportive it may have been to an unhealthy degree that only fuelled your negativity. You may decide that you are less tolerant of hanging around such negative influences. Equally, if you have been inclined to isolate yourself when feeling low, you might want to take the risk of telling someone how bad you feel and ask for help. On the other hand, a little solitude and duvet therapy when you feel vulnerable, might be just what you need as a wise decision to take care of yourself rather than expose yourself to others at a time when you cannot cope with it.

Some people like to create an altar, by that I mean a special place in their room, which acts as a focus for uplifting or spiritual thoughts. It can be a shelf or a table on which you place objects that symbolise something special to you. It might be a stone or a feather, it might be a candle and incense, or pictures of a spiritual teacher. It might even be a picture of you as a child. By tending your altar you are honouring the sacred in yourself and in life, sometimes celebrating the change of each season and its unique contribution to the cycle of the year. Creating an altar helps to bring a sense of sacredness and respect into your life and encourages you to treat yourself in a sacred way.

You may want to encourage the wild nature in yourself too by giving vent to some wild suggestions such as: dancing naked in front of a mirror, or in the moonlight, howling on top of a hill, or bathing naked in the sea.

Never underestimate the power of laughter. The famous American doctor and healer, Patch Adams, has made people realise the importance of humour in helping people not only to feel good, but also to help with their physical healing. Go out and have a really silly evening with friends, try and have at least one gut -busting moment when you laugh so uncontrollably that it is hard to breathe!

Whatever it is, continue to boost your morale, "love yourself up", say "No" to anything or anyone who tries to undermine you. You are the best medicine for your wellbeing. You are the source of your wellbeing; not others. If you learn to maintain it, no-one can take it away from you.

Allow yourself to be human, we all have "off days", we

do not have to be on top of the world all the time, we all do the same stupid things over and over again. Sometimes we do learn and sometimes, for no particular reason, life is just unfair and it really is not our fault. We are allowed to feel down, helpless and unable to cope sometimes, anyone would if they had to deal with the same situation. Whatever Life throws at us, whatever folly we face in ourselves; if we can hang on to our right to feel good about ourselves, we can regain our strength. If we can keep our heart open to ourselves and treat ourselves with love and compassion, then we will always have our self-esteem to sustain us. We will create a well of joy inside that we can draw on when we are thirsty; the well of our own being.

All of these are self-help techniques, things that you can do for yourself regardless of anyone else. However, as we learn to let go of our shame and our hate and as we learn to love ourselves, we also become more able to let in the love others have for us. I remember when I first began to let in that I mattered to others, even the friends I had treasured for years. I had always been aware of how much I loved and appreciated them and I was thankful for their tolerance and acceptance of me, but I realised that I had never really felt their love for me, I thought I had but I had blocked it out. It just did not compute with my view of myself. It is like feeling the warmth of the sun on your skin, to know that your friends love you just because they do.

❖

No More

All my life
I've been forced to fit where I don't
fit scissors, pens, cake-forks and cheque books
in a right-handed world
sinisterly
carrying the Lilith thing
the Jewish thing
the lesbian thing
the rogue and vagabond thespian thing
exposed invisible psychic creative thing

I was the unheard unseen
unacceptable inexplicable threat
who wanted only to belong

I learned your language tried to be nice
remembering not to ring
at five o' clock or ten- to- three
we the childless have to know these details
remembering always to ask
"how are the children? You must be proud"
and "that must be hard for you"
lose your company at half-term
When did you ever learn my language?
When did you ever consider the need?
All my life all my life I learned the script
the responses the gestures the look
but was there ever really any point
I was despite it all different

Now I stand in my own right
having learned to face the pain
own the rage
release the cynical humour
forgive and let go
made a bag of wisdom with it all
embroidered with magical hare and swan
and the exquisite cup of love I found
having filled it first with myself
Now I stand in my own light
and watch as the world comes to me
letting it pass by
welcoming those who want to stop and honour me

My spirit soars
for this is the time of the outsider
now the outside is in
and the inside fades to a better proportion
we're coming, we're here
as we always have been
the veil is off at last
watch out!

Bibliography

Maya Angelou *Collected Poems* "I Rise" "Phenomenal Woman"

Melodie Beatty *Codependent No More* Harper/Hazelden 1990
William Bloom *Feeling Safe, The Endorphin Effect* Piatkus 2001
John Bradshaw *Homecoming, Healing The Shame That Binds You*
Health Communications Inc. 1992

Julia Cameron *The Artist's Way* Tartcher/ Putnam 1992
Paul Coelho *The Alchemist* Thorsons 1995

Melanie Fennel *Overcoming Low Self-esteem* Constable and
Robinson 1999
Piero Ferrucci *What We May Be* Thorsons 1982

Elinor Gadon *The Once and Future Goddess* Aquarian Press 1990
John Firman and Ann Gila *Primal Wound* SUNY 1997

Susan Jeffries *Feel The Fear And Do It Anyway , The Little Book Of
Confidence* Rider
Kathy Jones *The Ancient British Goddess, Goddess Myths
Legends Sacred Sites and Present Revelations* Ariadne
Publications 2001.

Stephen Levine *Healing Into Life & Death* Doubleday 1989
Gael Lindenfield *Self Esteem* Harper Collins 2000

Pia Mellody (with Andrea and Keith Miller) *Facing Co-
dependence/ Breaking Free (workbook)* Harper & Row
1989, *Facing Love Addiction* Harper & Row 1992
Alice Miller *The Drama Of Being A Child* Virago Press 1987
Oriah Mountain Dreamer *The Invitation* Thorsons 1999

Clarissa Pinkola Estes *Women Who Run With The Wolves* Rider 1992

Robin Skynner & John Cleese *Families and How to Survive Them* Methuen 1983

Tina Turner *I Tina* Penguin 1987

Alice Walker *The Colour Purple* Women's Press 2001
D W Winnicott *Playing and Reality* Penguin 1988

Marion Zimmer Bradley *The Mists of Avalon* Penguin 1983, *Priestess of Avalon* Penguin

Index

Contacting the Author

Rachael Clyne can be contacted via her website:

www.sweet-track-counselling.co.uk

Sweet Track Counselling Services

Spiritual Counselling Training

Certificate in Counselling Skills (CPCAB)

*For those who wish to combine
their psychic and spiritual awareness
with counselling skills and ethical practice*

*A one-year accredited training
in spiritual counselling skills
in Glastonbury*

with
Rachael Clyne & Collette Barnard

There are many people who use counselling skills in their work and who wish to draw on their psychic and intuitive abilities in order to address the spiritual world of their clients. And there are those who wish to ground their psychic and intuitive work with counselling skills and ethical practice. This course aims to bring these two very important aspects together.

The course is run via the Isle of Avalon Foundation:
c/o 2-4 High Street, Glastonbury, BA6 9DU.

For more information contact their address via the website:
www.isleofavalonfoundation.com

alternatively contact:
www.sweet-track-counselling.co.uk

PS AVALON PUBLISHING

About PS Avalon

PS Avalon Publishing is an independent and committed publisher offering a complete publishing service, including editorial, manuscript preparation, printing, promotion, marketing and distribution. As a small publisher enabled to take full advantage of the latest technological advances, PS Avalon Publishing can offer an alternative route for aspiring authors working in our particular fields of interest.

As well as publishing, we offer a comprehensive education programme including courses, seminars, group retreats, and other opportunities for personal and spiritual growth. Whilst the nature of our work means we engage with people from all around the world, we are based in Glastonbury which is in the West Country of England.

new poetry books

Our purpose is to bring you the best new poetry with a psychospiritual content. Our intent is to make poetry relevant again, offering work that is contemplative and inspirational, with a dark, challenging edge.

self development books

We publish inspiring reading material aimed at enhancing your life development without overburdening you with too many words. Everything is kept as simple and as accessible as possible.

journals

With its full colour design, easy on-line availability, and most of all with its exciting and inspiring contents, *The Synthesist* journal is a popular offering to the psychospiritual world and beyond.

PS AVALON PUBLISHING
Box 1865, Glastonbury,
Somerset BA6 8YR, U.K.

www.psavalon.com

info@psavalon.com

Printed in the United Kingdom
by Lightning Source UK Ltd.
130500UK00002BB/85/A